MATYA
FOREWORD B'

GN00986744

TRANS
STRUCTURES

FLUID ARCHITECTURE AND LIQUID ENGINEERING
RESPONSE-ABLE INNOVATIVE STRUCTURES

GRAPHIC DESIGN BY LILIANA RODRIGUES // ILLUSTRATIONS BY ARIS KAFANTARIS
ACADEMIC EDITING BY ZOHEIR MOTTAKI

Trans Structures
Fluid Architecture and Liquid Engineering.
Response-able Innovative Structures

Author and editor
Matyas Gutai

Published by
Actar Publishers
New York, 2014

Graphic Designer
Liliana Rodrigues

Illustrations
Aris Kafantaris

Academic Editing
Zoheir Mottaki

ISBN 978-1-940291-44-4
A CIP catalogue record for this book is
available from the Library of Congress,
Washington D.C., USA.

Distributed by
Actar D, New York
www.actar-d.com

New York
355 Lexington Avenue, 8th Floor
New York, NY 10017
T +1 212 966 2207
F +1 212 966 2214
salesnewyork@actar-d.com

Barcelona
Roca i Batlle 2
08023 Barcelona
salesbarcelona@actar-d.com
eurosales@actar-d.com

CONTENTS

FOREWORD

1960's Japan gave birth to the architectural movement called "Metabolism." It was the way of thinking that architecture could metabolize itself as a living organism, which can adapt to environmental changes. Kisho Kurokawa, as well as other architects of the movement, thought to realize this idea by means of making architecture as a collection of replaceable capsules or units, and exchanging them with new ones as needed.

These capsules however, intended as the metabolism architecture, have in reality never been renewed after construction. "Metabolism" was the conceptual stimulus and attracted attention from the world, but the movement remained largely an unrealized idea. It is therefore hard to say that the idea was realistic, and the movement did not change the world. One possible hint for this conceptual failure is that "Metabolism" viewed life based on the unit of the organ, with life as a collection of these organs. In the 20th century, this mentality predominated; even the Japanese architectural avant-garde was also preoccupied with this model.

Seen from a different perspective, life is not only a collection of organs. We are starting to think that an organ is already too large and complex to be a unit. We are now starting to think of life based on much smaller things. But the problem is not only one of size. It is the most important point in modern view, that life is not simply a collection of units, but instead a stream, a thing streaming. This idea is not only for advanced scientists. This notion, that life is a stream and that we ourselves are streaming, is already a very universal idea that pervades our daily life, invisibly.

Matyas Gutai's concept "Trans-structure" is integral to this new view of life: for him, architecture is not a collection of units, but a stream. A thing that is streaming can change itself easily. Rather, it would be hard and unnatural for such things to remain still.

This book thus focuses on architecture as a streaming, living thing.

Kengo Kuma
4th September 2014 Tokyo

PART
ONE

ON TRANS-STRUCTURES

TRANSI-
TION

Busan Cinema Center, stage area
© COOP HIMMELB(L)AU

TRANSITION:
STABILITY OF CHANGE

Stability is a fundamental characteristic of building since the dawn of architecture practice and discourse, starting with the Vitruvian 'firmitas'. Maintaining a relatively unchanged state of structure and indoor environment is essential and primary function of every building still today. Stability is not only an issue of material, construction or esthetic preference but also about indoor comfort and permanent thermal quality. These two aspects of construction and comfort may seem very different, yet the problem of unchanged state was always solved based on the same strategy in the past for both. The keyword was cumulative strength and passive resistance, achieved by additional materials. This assured stronger construction, and also higher resistance against external heating-cooling effects. The long history of this strategy might have led the misconception that strong is stable. These two aspects of stability are also connected by energy as a mutual value. Life Cycle Assessment refers to both operational demand and embedded energy for material provision and manufacture. Their union however also shows the limitations of current low energy building methods: more matter can lower operational energy demands, but since it causes the embedded energy to increase, the total impact for the whole life cycle remains high.

THIS CONNECTION BETWEEN EMBODIED AND CONSUMED ENERGY SUGGESTS THAT LIMITS WILL LIKELY REMAIN EVEN IN THE FUTURE, REGARDLESS OF FURTHER TECHNICAL IMPROVEMENT OR THE ADVENT OF NEW MATERIALS; WE HAVE TO INVEST IN ONE IN ORDER TO MITIGATE THE OTHER. HOWEVER, THIS CORRELATION IS ONLY RESULTED BY THE SOLID AND PASSIVE STATE OF THE STRUCTURE, BECAUSE MATERIALS WITH INTRINSICALLY DIFFERENT PROPERTIES CAN ELIMINATE THIS DRAWBACK, DUE TO THE FACT THAT THE PROBLEM IS WITH THE DESIGN MODEL AND NOT WITH THE STRUCTURE.

The same goes for the state of change itself. No matter how resistant or strong the structure is, passive properties cannot defy the inevitable changes of environment forever. Without external energy investment, the interior will inevitably obey the forces of nature and will change as exterior dictates. Again, technical development or new materials are not the key to solve this dilemma, if they follow the same model. These tectonic and technical features might be capable to minimize the energy need further, but are unable to eliminate it, since stable and unchanged state cannot be based upon passive properties alone. Changing the passive resistance of the structure therefore appears to be an inadequate solution. "We cannot solve our problems with the same thinking we used when we created them." [1].

One might question the possibility of changing the model as an alternative. The question sounds logical, however the answer is quite difficult, especially because sustainable design so far, did not change our architecture as fundamentally when it comes to the model of stability, and our buildings are based on the same stability assumptions. Sustainability changed building technology, engineering and construction; it influenced and inspired even architecture and design, but so far did not address the way we maintain an unchanged state.

AS AN ALTERNATIVE SOLUTION, REAL STABILITY COMES WITH RESPONSE-ABILITY,

WHEN ANY "EFFECT" (STRUCTURAL OR THERMAL LOAD) CAN BE COUNTERACTED WITH AN IMMEDIATE "AFFECT" THAT IS AN APPROPRIATE RESPONSE OF THE STRUCTURE. ENERGY AND LOAD COULD BE COUNTERACTED AND ON A TOTAL SCALE, CHANGE WOULD NOT OCCUR.

When it comes to energy, conventional structures performance is comparable to a spaceship: the goal generally is to create a perfect barrier between outside and inside to minimize energy exchange and operational demands at the same time. Trans-structure is the opposite: it is in constant transition to embrace environmental changes, like the nomads move for greenery on land and the surfers for waves on water[2]. Resembling to the way of Aikido, Trans-structure takes control of external forces, using them in its advantage instead opposing them. It is expressed elegantly in Budo Martial Arts: "The best strategy relies on unlimited responses.".[3]

A structure like that would not have a static state, neither in sense of energy nor of matter: it would be heavy some cases and light in others depending on the actual structural demands; also it would be warm or cold according to the requirements of the microclimate. On the scale of the whole structure, its own weight and contained energy could be dispersed in different way each time, defined by actual conditions and demands. Such structure is never a stable one, to be able to assure real stability. In this respect, the structure is always in transition from one state to another, which is the most important essence of Trans-structure.

Trans-structure with its perpetual change can assure the state of "dynamic stability", which is not only essential for self-sustainability, but also can transcend the limits of sustainability into inspiration for architectural design. This dynamic structural state however requires us to redefine the basic principles in engineering, because our current technologies rely on static systems only.

Busan Cinema Center designed by COOP Himmelblau is a good example to show the potential of this thinking. The spectacular 85 meter long cantilevered roof could not have been built based on conventional engineering: since typhoon winds are getting stronger, the structure was simply not sufficient anymore to resist the new design criteria, which was introduced after the construction has already started. In case of reconstruction, the necessary foundation and vertical core would have been too massive to build. It may sound controversial to design a building based on a load that occurs once a year for a short period, especially when it determines the faith of the whole architectural concept. In case of classic engineering and design however, it is exactly the case, because the conventional strategy of stability excludes any possibility of change and adaptation.

To overcome this difficulty, additional columns have been added to the structure, which only rise from basement when typhoon winds pass through Korea. This unique solution was based upon the recognition that a shift from a rigid and closed structural design to an open system has the potential to provide novel pertinent possibilities in architecture and building.

Busan Cinema Center, street view
© COOP HIMMELB(L)AU

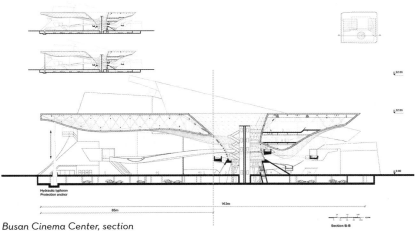

Hydraulic typhoon
Protection anchor

85m

163m

Section B-B

Busan Cinema Center, section
© COOP HIMMELB(L)AU

TRANS-STRUCTURES ARE BASED
ON THE SAME PRINCIPLE;
THE BALANCE IS ASSURED BY
THE RESPONSE (CHANGE)
OF THE STRUCTURE.
NATURALLY, THE CAPACITY
OF CHANGE ITSELF IS
NOT SUFFICIENT:
THE RESPONSE ALSO HAS TO

BE IMMEDIATE AND ADEQUATE.

The former is the problem of material. We have been consuming materials of the earth throughout history. Solid matters are relatively slow-paced due to their nature. This could be the reason, why architecture was anchored to the concept of strength. Trans-structures therefore cannot be based on solids only. In order to achieve effective response-ability, fluid and gas materials have to be 'Architecturalized', in order to create structures with novel properties.

At first glance, the challenge of adequate response appears to be a problem of technology, especially in light of more recent examples utilizing high-tech solutions to create adapting built environments and architecture. Compared with those examples, Trans-structures have an important difference. Smart systems only "act," in the sense, that certain predefined conditions trigger a desired effect (as in the case of increased sunlight, a shading device is activated).

The result is however rarely enough to maintain thermal comfort. Responsive environments "react", which means that the system generates alterations in the form of new manner modes to achieve the desired effect (like cooling indoors when temperature rises), but the system relies on external sources to maintain the stability. Trans-structure however provides the exact "response" (unchanged state based on inverse countermeasures of external and internal environmental loads). If all the changes in environment and indoors are united in one "Effect" and the response can be defined as "Affect," then in case of Trans-structure, the union of the two equals zero, and change would not occur.

The ultimate outcome is similar to Responsive Environments with the distinction in the source of change or counter-effects that, Trans-structure is not an external source but the building itself. In other words, for the former, smart technology is required while for the latter, the smart is indeed the structure itself. To accomplish this mission, a new type of control system is necessary, which allows the structure to generate immediate and adequate responses. This is mainly achieved through possible reactions that affect multiple structural properties.

Physical and thermal loads both correspondingly define the actual state of the structure, and they remain connected: a higher mass generated to resist strong winds for instance, also results in higher thermal mass and slower responses for cooling-heating at simultaneously.

Consequently, Trans-structures require not only novel materials, but also a new model for control system, which can result in a dynamic structural behavior, and is also capable to cope with the interrelations of simultaneous thermal and structural loads.

---

[1] Quote from Albert Einstein

[2] J. Reiser, N. Umemoto: Atlas of Novel Tectonics, Princeton Architectural Press, New York, 2006

[3] M. Ueshiba: Budo: Teachings of the Founder of Aikido, Kodansha America Inc., New York, 1991

INTER-
RELA-
TION

MATRIX OF STILL STANDING

INTERRELATION
MATRIX OF STILL STANDING

Manmade stability and longevity is based on the illusion of strength, however when it comes to Nature, it is more based on adaptability and continuous change. Biologist J. Scott Turner explains this difference with the 'Bernard machine' [1], based on the work of Darwin's contemporary, Claude Bernard. In contrast to the concept of Darwinism on evolution, the Bernard model emphasizes the importance of change and versatility as a definitive force in our living environment. In the case of Trans-structure, the Bernard model is principally essential because homeostasis shows how a system "defined by constant adjustment process" can provide a considerably more effective and accommodating structure than current Engineering Methods based on passive measures.

Turner explains that bone homeostasis is regulated by the cooperation of two different cells: osteocytes and osteoclasts. The former is responsible for building and strengthening the structure. The latter is the opposite: removing calcium and phosphate to return them to the blood. This cooperation assures the bone to be a dynamic structure in a constant cycle of building up and deconstruction for optimized performance.

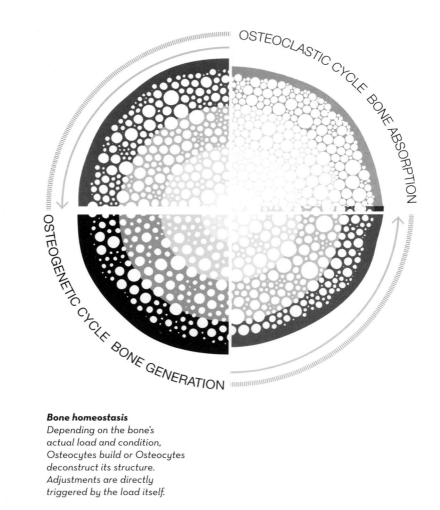

OSTEOCLASTIC CYCLE BONE ABSORPTION

OSTEOGENETIC CYCLE BONE GENERATION

Bone homeostasis

*Depending on the bone's
actual load and condition,
Osteocytes build or Osteocytes
deconstruct its structure.
Adjustments are directly
triggered by the load itself.*

The dynamic stability of homeostasis works without any central control system, since any change is generated directly by the bone's actual load and condition. Osteocytes monitor the structure continuously and their action is determined by the strains in the bone. As soon as the bone becomes weak and the strains increase, osteocytes increase the density of the bones to reduce the strains again. In case of the opposite, the osteocytes simply allow the osteoclasts to take over and deconstruct the bone structure until ideal balance can be reached. "Structure is matched elegantly to function, and everywhere the bone is optimally bearing its load. Thus, it is not genetic specification – a Darwin machine – that is responsible for the bone's good design, but a Bernard machine – the osteocytes' capability for the strain homeostasis. In a profound sense, bones are well designed because they want to be well designed. They 'know' when their design falls short, and they take active steps to remedy the shortcomings." [2]

Direct connection between bone stress and remodeling is essential for Trans-structure's design as well. Unlike smart structures or materials, homeostasis does not rely on external decision-making process. The cause of change triggers the reaction directly, eliminating any need of interaction, monitoring or additional energy provision. The possibility of immediate responses depends on the choice of material and state of matter: unlike solids, both fluid or gas can provide inherent responsiveness for the structure. Control is an equally crucial obstacle because a structure or building envelope is much more than just an object of its own; and thereby cannot be potentially investigated in isolated conditions. Rather it has to be examined in state of 'ceaseless flux', described by Johan Wolfgang von Goethe. To him it is possible to generate morphology while leaving the Aristotelian view behind in order to create an approach that takes the dynamic interactions of the whole into account: "when we study forms, the organic ones in particular, nowhere do we find permanence, repose or termination. We find rather that everything is in ceaseless flux. This is why our language makes such frequent use of the term 'Building' to designate what has been brought forth and likewise what is in the process of being brought forth." [3]

When it comes to a structure, the problem of stability (not only material sense but also energy) relies on dynamic relationship of 'Effects' (generated by environment) and 'Affects' (response of the structure). Just as Effects are collection of variables with myriads of possible combinations, so are the 'Affects' as well, and thereby the holistic system generates an interrelation matrix between variables of actions and responses.

TO ESTABLISH AN EFFECTIVE RESPONSE-ABLE SYSTEM, EXTERNAL MONITORING SOLELY IS NOT SUFFICIENT: CEASELESS FLUX HAS TO BE MAINTAINED BY DIRECT RELATIONSHIP BETWEEN CAUSE AND OUTCOME, JUST LIKE IN NATURE.

Although being collection of objects, structure is described here as a system, in the same way as Christopher Alexander defined it: an Abstraction. In 'Systems Generating Systems' he uses the example of candle flame to present a holistic phenomenon, where different variables are in continuous interaction until a balance can be reached. According to Alexander: "The most important properties which anything can have are those properties that deal with its stability. It is stability, which gives a thing its essential character." [4]

Natural models of stability are not limited to singular variables, like strength of bones. In case of Chloroplast movement for example, the reactions are controlled by heat and insolation. Chloroplasts are responsible for photosynthesis, but because their solar exposure is limited to a certain level, they are in constant motion for ideal solar gain and radiation. Chloroplast movement and solar irradiance are in direct correlation: Sunlight itself triggers the motion and angle of the cell subunits and speed is always proportional to the solar gain.

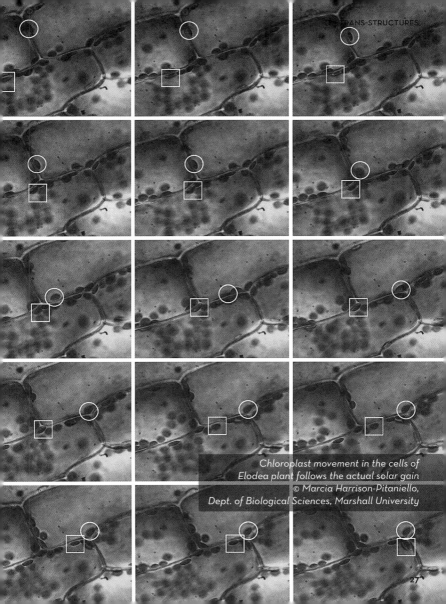

Chloroplast movement in the cells of
Elodea plant follows the actual solar gain
© *Marcia Harrison-Pitaniello,*
Dept. of Biological Sciences, Marshall University

27

'Gravitropism', which assures plants to grow vertically, is another example of this direct control. A special hormone, auxin is produced in the cells at the tip of the steam and below the hook area. The auxin moves constantly downwards in the steam, stimulating the cells to grow. In case the plant falls are in horizontal state, more auxin is transported to the cells on the lower side to grow more rapidly. The interaction of auxin with environmental and chemical signals assures not only vertical growth but also orientation towards the sun: In case of asymmetric light, auxin moves towards the shaded area of the plant (Cholodny-Went hypothesis) [5] and generates phototropism.

Compared to nature's open and resilient control, technology always operates in predetermined and predefined conditions. Ludwig von Bertalanffy describes the two aspects as 'dynamic' and 'machinelike' in 'General System Theory: Foundations, Development, Applications'. Dynamic systems are described as potential source of the predetermined; since the generated responses of the general can be source of fixed constraints in future design. [6] This was the case of any conventional structural design in the past. The fact, that the resulted model became passive and free of any dynamism in the process, was of little importance, since the utilized solids were free of responsive properties.

Gravitropism assures vertical growth of plants
without external or central control system
© Marcia Harrison-Pitaniello,
Dept. of Biological Sciences, Marshall University

Trans-structure is between the two: union of inherent responsive materials and structural passive solids. The first experimental model of such system was designed and built in professor Kazuhiko Namba's laboratory at the University of Tokyo, Faculty of Architecture. The environmental tests have been conducted at the Budapest University of Technology, Department of Architecture, in the laboratory of Building Physics. Prof. Jeno Kontra and Prof. Janos Varfalvi led the research in Europe. The model was a hybrid structure: union of water and lightweight solid volume. The proportions were of a typical room in scale of 1:3.

Water volumes were connected all around the section of the room and free flow was assured between vertical and horizontal areas. The fluid infill formed one coherent water volume in the whole structure.

The goal of the experiment was to prove that even a small amount of water volume could be an effective heat regulator without constant programing or external control, and thereby generate a Trans-structure system.

A BUILDING LIKE THIS WOULD BE MUCH MORE THAN A SIMPLE HYBRID CONSTRUCTION: THE INTERCONNECTED STRUCTURAL ELEMENTS WOULD WORK TOGETHER LIKE THE THERMODYNAMIC MODEL OF PLANET EARTH, IN WHICH, THE UNION OF MASS (SOIL), INSULATION (AIR) AND DISTRIBUTION (WATER) CREATES CEASELESS FLUX AND STABLE ATMOSPHERE.

THE ONLY DIFFERENCE IS THE FACT THAT WHAT WOULD TAKE ONE YEAR ON PLANETARY SCALE WOULD TAKE ONLY SECONDS IN A BUILDING.

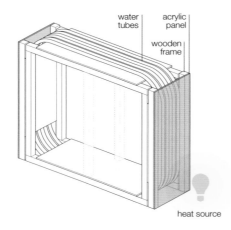

water tubes | acrylic panel
wooden frame

heat source

Water House experiment.
Joint research project of The University of Tokyo and Budapest University of Technology and Economics.

The experiment exposes the model for 80 minutes to a constant heating source at one vertical side of the structure. The heat-gain side started to warm up, but after the first phase, the temperature started to drop without any change on the other side.

In the next phase both sides started to warm up as the thermal storage reached its maximum limit in the whole section.

In the final stages the exposed side continues to experience recurring temperature increases and drops, while the other side warms continuously until a final balance was reached.

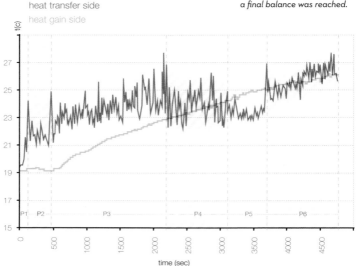

heat transfer side
heat gain side

THE CREATED HYBRID WAS THE FIRST SYSTEM THAT WAS CAPABLE TO SHOW THE MAIN CHARACTERISTICS OF A TRANS-STRUCTURE: IMMEDIATE AND ADEQUATE RESPONSES AGAINST AN EXTERNAL EFFECT (1) MAINTAINED BALANCE OF CEASELESS FLUX AND TRANSITION OF STATES (2) BASED ON INHERENT MATERIAL RESPONSIVENESS PARTIALLY OBVIATING EXTERNAL PROGRAMING OR CONTROL (3).

The capacity of change in case of a hybrid structure of solid-fluid is not obviously limited only to thermal storage capacity. Fluid can move in and out from the shell just as easily, similarly to the experiment model. A wall panel structure with changing water content could be fabricated just as easily, in which the water volumes (thickness in the wall) can be changed. A structure like that would be able to change mass, thermal storage capacity, and transparency at any time based on external effects. In the Trans-structure diagram shown here, each state is represented with four main axes.
The first is 'Storer-Consumer', which refers to the energy absorbed in the actual state, and the energy consumed at the same time (storage process also requires limited amount of energy investment).

***Typical state of a
Trans-structure***
*in winter (above)
and summer (below)*

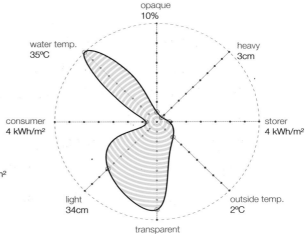

(storer) St: 4 kWh/m²
(consumer) Co: 4 kWh/m²
(water temp) Wt: 35°C
(outside temp) Ot: 2°C
(water volume) Wv: 3cm
(air volume) Av: 34cm
(opaque) Op: 10%
(transparent) Tr: 90%

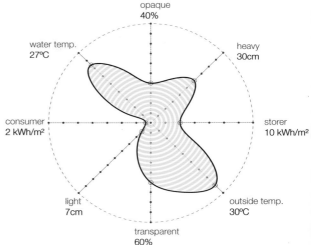

(storer) St: 10 kWh/m²
(consumer) Co: 2 kWh/m²
(water temp) Wt: 27°C
(outside temp) Ot: 30°C
(water volume) Wv: 30cm
(air volume) Av: 7cm
(opaque) Op: 40%
(transparent) Tr: 60%

The second is Heating/Cooling-Temperature, showing the radiated energy of structural surface in relation to the external temperature. The third is Transparency-Opacity of the building envelope, which can also change as well (as we will see in the Pattern Panel project). Trans-structure diagram shows four different typical states for both winter and summer: Storage (heat is absorbed and sent to external storage), Balance (heat is absorbed and thermal mass is sufficient), Radiant (heat surplus is returned to exterior) and Cooling/Heating modes (external energy is utilized to maintain stability).

Naturally, these states are only representative momentums of a constant flux. Since the changes are always proportional to the environmental effects, the numbers of possible states are almost unlimited. Trans-structure diagram is therefore a volume of constant flux rather than the collection of individual elements, similar to the holistic capacity of the structure itself.

---

[1] J Scott Turner: Evolutionary Architecture? Some Perspectives From Biological Design, in Achim Menges (ed.): Material Computation: Higher Integration in Morphogenetic Design, page 28-33, John Wiley & Sons, London 2012

[2] Ibid. Page 35.

[3] J. W. von Goethe: Formation and Transformation, translated by Bertha Mueller, in A. Menges and S. Ahlquist (ed.): Computational Design Thinking, page 31, John Wiley and Sons, London, 2011

[4] C. Alexander: Systems Generating Systems, in in A. Menges and S. Ahlquist (ed.): Computational Design Thinking, page 60, John Wiley and Sons, London, 2011

[5] Christie, J.M., and Murphy, A.S. (2013). Shoot phototropism in higher plants: New light through old concepts. American Journal of Botany 100(1), 35-46

[6] L. von Bertanalffy: General Systems Theory: Foundations, Development, Applications, George Braziller, New York, 1969

*Changes of Trans-structure
in winter*

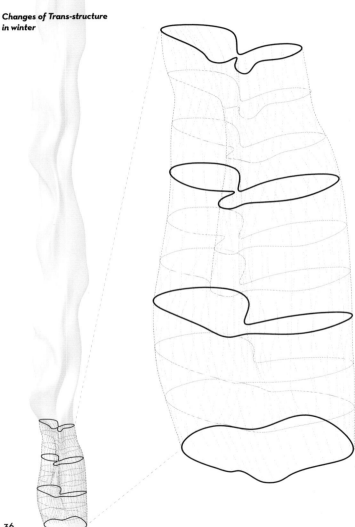

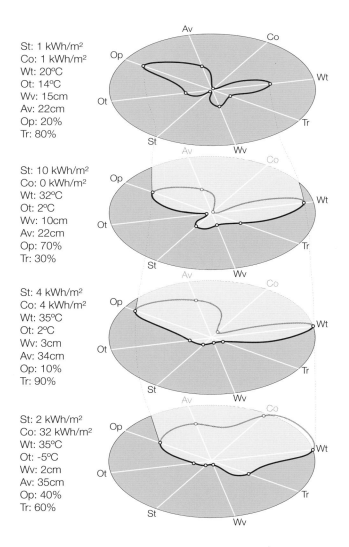

St: 1 kWh/m²
Co: 1 kWh/m²
Wt: 20°C
Ot: 14°C
Wv: 15cm
Av: 22cm
Op: 20%
Tr: 80%

St: 10 kWh/m²
Co: 0 kWh/m²
Wt: 32°C
Ot: 2°C
Wv: 10cm
Av: 22cm
Op: 70%
Tr: 30%

St: 4 kWh/m²
Co: 4 kWh/m²
Wt: 35°C
Ot: 2°C
Wv: 3cm
Av: 34cm
Op: 10%
Tr: 90%

St: 2 kWh/m²
Co: 32 kWh/m²
Wt: 35°C
Ot: -5°C
Wv: 2cm
Av: 35cm
Op: 40%
Tr: 60%

**Changes of Trans-structure
in summer**

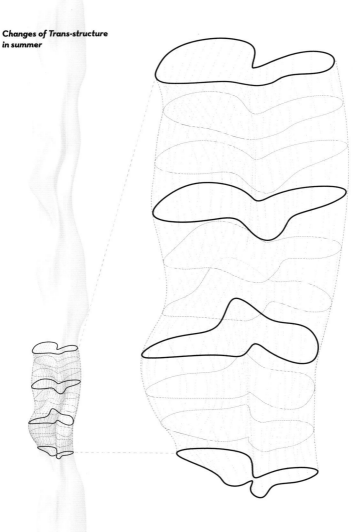

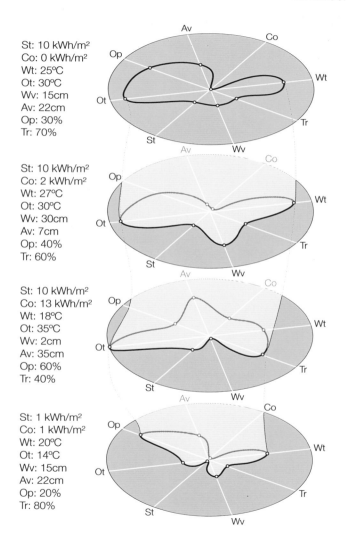

St: 10 kWh/m²
Co: 0 kWh/m²
Wt: 25°C
Ot: 30°C
Wv: 15cm
Av: 22cm
Op: 30%
Tr: 70%

St: 10 kWh/m²
Co: 2 kWh/m²
Wt: 27°C
Ot: 30°C
Wv: 30cm
Av: 7cm
Op: 40%
Tr: 60%

St: 10 kWh/m²
Co: 13 kWh/m²
Wt: 18°C
Ot: 35°C
Wv: 2cm
Av: 35cm
Op: 60%
Tr: 40%

St: 1 kWh/m²
Co: 1 kWh/m²
Wt: 20°C
Ot: 14°C
Wv: 15cm
Av: 22cm
Op: 20%
Tr: 80%

DUAL CYCLE

HYBRYD AND FUSION

DUAL CYCLE
HYBRID AND FUSION

The dilemma of choice between Light and Heavy for building is inevitable in solid constructions. Both options have their advantages: the first is preferred for lower initial demand for material, energy, waste or pollution, while the second provides thermal comfort and energy savings in the long term. The difference between the two options however is not always as substantial as it may seem. This is due to the fact that embedded energy of materials is not related to their weight, and in addition, a minimal mass is always required for additional reasons (i.e. fire safety or acoustics), even if stability allows lighter structure.

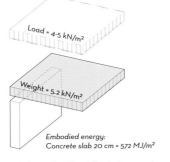

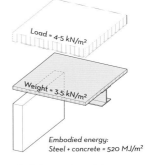

Embodied energy of light and heavy structure

Embodied energy:
Concrete slab 20 cm = 572 MJ/m²

Embodied energy:
Steel + concrete = 520 MJ/m²

Weight may be different for steel or concrete construction, embodied energy does not change proportionally. Trans-structure's medium is made by natural materials (air or water) which lowers embodied energy considerably.

TRANS-STRUCTURE CHANGES ITS STATE BASED ON ACTUAL LOADS AND THEREFORE THE INEVITABLE CHOICE OF LIGHT OR HEAVYBUILDING SIMPLY DOES NOT EXIST. SOLID CONSTRUCTIONS ARE LIMITED TO PREDETERMINED CONDITIONS OR PASSIVE STATE, BUT FOR HYBRID SYSTEMS, LIGHTNESS OR HEAVINESS ARE ONLY TWO STATES AMONG MANY OTHERS.

Naturally, mass in structure is crucial for both load-bearing capacity and thermal comfort, and the former requires less material than the latter, eventhough mass demand of stable microclimate changes all the time. These differences are not important factors when it comes to solid building methods, since the material presence is constant after completion. It is however essential for Trans-structures as mass varies from one state to the other.

Trans-structure's building elements belong to two separate groups: core and medium. Core is typically solid material, and is responsible for constant properties of the structure (like geometry). Medium is typically utilized to assure the capacity of change: modify the mass from light to heavy, or switch envelope from state of energy storage to consumption. Mediums are liquids or gases for effective responsiveness and distribution. The changing mass of medium provides the additional thermal storage for stable microclimate as well. Depending on the state of medium and the source of additional energy sources, Trans-structure can be achieved in various ways.

In case of Hybrids, the medium is embedded into the structure. The weight changes during building process: light during construction and heavy in operation. Total mass remains constant in the building, but the main difference compared to solid structures is, that hybrid mediums are effective distributors. For any local demand or load, the whole structure integratedly reacts, that is the fluid volume of the whole building works as one capacity. This way even in case of a thin local mass, the structure is superior compared to a heavy solid construction, because any effect deals with the thermal capacity of the whole building, regardless the location or affected area. Here, the necessary extra mass is therefore assured by the effective distribution. Connected to conventional heat storage and heating-cooling devices, Hybrids work like a heat trap; storing heat surplus for later use to minimize heating energy consumption. 'Allwater' and Tea-Water Pavilions introduced in Part Three work exactly this way.

Trans-structure, *first based on effective distribution of medium and second on union with external mass*

HYBRID

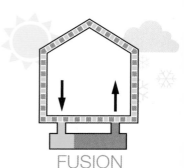

FUSION

Another method is Fusion, when Trans-structure is fused with surroundings to increase thermal storage capacity. Stone plants (Lithops) in South Africa follow this method [1] : heat is captured by the soil surrounding the plant in the ground during the day, and the same heat is reused to keep it warm in the evening. The plant in this manner could have considerably less mass itself, while still capable to capture the necessary heat in cooperation with the immediate environment. Trans-structure cores are lightweight, and in case of Fusion the medium as well, because the main mass of the building is practically the surroundings. 'Meme Meadows' project, shown in Part Two of this book, is a good example for this model.

ALTHOUGH HYBRID AND FUSION MODELS DIFFER IN VARIOUS WAYS, BOTH TRANS-STRUCTURE TYPES ARE CAPABLE TO UNITE THE ADVANTAGES OF LIGHT AND HEAVY BUILDING: EASY ASSEMBLY AND LARGE THERMAL MASS; WITH EMBEDDED RESPONSIVENESS BASED ON MATERIAL PROPERTIES WHILE OBVIATING THE CONSTANT NEED FOR MONITORING OR PROGRAMMED CONTROL.

The duality of Core and Medium in Trans-structures is beyond merely a solution for light-heavy building system. In addition it is also the coalescence of natural and artificial matter and thereby brings architecture closer to the constructs of nature: "Biological materials are constructed at ambient temperatures and use only two polymers (protein and polysaccharide), with two ceramics (calcium salts and silica) and a few metals, whereas human-made materials require high temperatures and hundreds of polymers. Most significantly, biological materials contain water, a component that is missing from nearly all human-made materials and which viewed in that context as an agent of degradation." [2]

More importantly, the two constituents of Trans-structure refer to different structural functions and thus remain separated at all times. This affects efficiency of material use and waste production. The first important advantage is, that solid core is always a light structure and its function is limited to loadbearing and rigidity, without taking additional criteria (like thermal comfort) into account. This offers more freedom in design or material choice, and allows effective recycling at low embedded energy cost. This fresh freedom thereby brings an opportunity to design structures similar to nature, where "materials are expensive and shape is cheap, as opposed to technology where the opposite tends to be the case." [3]

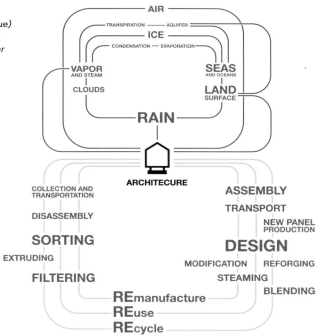

Dual Cycle
of Natural (blue)
and Industrial
(yellow) matter

Conventional building methods are not only involved with solids, but also limited in source: "The basic materials in the history of architecture – stone, brick, wood and metals – all derive from earth and these materials re-unite building back to the earth and its processes." [4]

Trans-structures however are neither one: by introducing building principles of nature, they bring a new paradigm in architecture and sustainable design.

NATURE MINIMIZES MATERIAL USE WITH FORM AND
ADAPTABILITY, WHILE UTILIZES SOLIDS WITH WATER
AND GAS FOR ITS STRUCTURES. CONSTRUCTION AND
DECONSTRUCTION OCCURS IN NATURAL ENVIRONMENT
(AMBIENT TEMPERATURE, PRESSURE, ETC.), SO THAT
'WASTE ALWAYS EQUALS FOOD'. HOWEVER MANMADE
ON THE OPPOSITE IS LIMITED TO SOLIDS WITH PASSIVE
DESIGN, OVER-SCALED MATERIAL USE, AND MATERIAL
PRODUCTION IN ARTIFICIAL CONDITIONS. TRANS-
STRUCTURES ARE BOTH: THE UNION OF SOLID AND
GAS/WATER EACH RESPONSIBLE FOR DIFFERENT
STRUCTURAL FUNCTIONS, WITH RECYCLABLE
INDUSTRIAL SOLIDS AND NATURAL COMPONENTS,
WHICH ARE KEPT SEPARATED FOR A DUAL MATERIAL
CYCLE, WHERE MATERIALS ARE ONLY BESTOWED
UPON ARCHITECTURE.

"Nature has no design problem. People do." [5], perhaps partially because the desire for unnatural microclimate, where nothing changes. An architecture based on a purely natural model is therefore extremely difficult to achieve. Trans-structures are however an important step in that direction to aim for a more sustainable architecture in the future.

---

[1] Described in R. Allen (ed.): Bulletproof feathers: how science uses nature's secrets to design cutting edge technology, University of Chicago Press, London, 2010

[2] Ibid. pp. 134.

[3] J. F. V. Vincent and P. Owners, "Mechanical design of hedgehog spines and porcupine quills", Journal of Zoology 210, 1986. pp.55-75

[4] R. McCarter, J. Pallasmaa: Understanding Architecture, page 81, Phaidon Press, London, 2012

[5] W. McDonough, M. Braungart: Cradle to Cradle, page 4, North Point Press, New York, 2002

MULTI
FUNC-
TION

UNITY AND COMPLEXITY

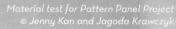

Material test for Pattern Panel Project
© Jenny Kan and Jagoda Krawczyk

MULTIFUNCTION
UNITY AND COMPLEXITY

The division of 'material' and 'structure' was an invention of the 20th century. Architecture utilized multifunctional elements before the Modern Era: a stone or brick wall was not only structure for both load-bearing and rigidity, but also thermal mass and insulation when required, and additionally, it was even the finish in many cases. The terms 'structure' and 'matter' conveyed the same meaning, and buildings stood bare leaving little doubt about how to build them.

With the dawn of the First Machine Age everything changed. Industrialization redefined both engineering and construction. A simple wall became a collection of independent elements: external finish, insulation, load-bearing frame, veneer infill and interior wall finish for example. Matter and technology was connected directly to the role of the actual element as part of the whole, rather than to the structure itself.

BUILDING WAS SEEN AS COLLECTION OF ISOLATED MONOFUNCTIONAL PRODUCTS, INSTEAD OF BEING A HOLISTIC STRUCTURAL ENTITY. COMPLEXITY OF 'STRUCTURAL BEHAVIOR' WAS REPLACED BY COMPLEXITY OF 'FORMAL ASSEMBLY'.

This development made sense in many ways, since isolated components had higher market viability and engineering design could cope up more easily with the increased technical demand. On the other hand, accumulated elements increased not only complexity but also compromised each other's efficiency. Products are designed in isolated and ideal conditions and therefore become inevitably compromised when they have to meet the given conditions of an actual project: either solar panels for instance control the design for ideal insolation or they operate on lower efficiency. Additionally, such an accumulation differentiated the lifespan of the building elements, which increased the embedded energy of the total life cycle as a result. Sustainability changed this process to certain extent, but also to meet the demands of energy-efficiency and use of renewables for instance, new elements and technologies had to be added to the structure.

PREMODERN   FIRST MACHINE AGE

ENERGY

distribution
heating
cooling

THERMAL MASS

thermal mass
absorption
time-lag
insulation

SKIN

transparency
rigidity
load bearing
resistance
isolation
enclosure
shading
illumination
ornament
finish

VENTILATION

natural
exhaust
intake

OPENING

door
window

SECOND MACHINE AGE

TRANS-STRUCTURE

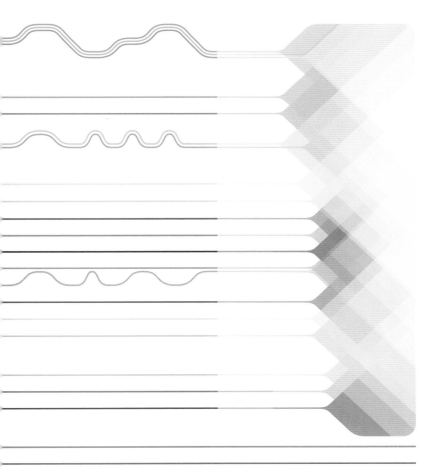

Mono-function and Multifunction *of building envelope elements*

This clear mono-functionality however already started to vanish in the end of the First Machine Age. Reyner Banham presented structures such as Pompidou;[1] where engineering takes over other fields of architecture and after long time, building elments show first signs of multi-functionality as a part of load-bearing structure or building envelope. This continues in the Second Machine Age, when one particular structural or engineering system became responsible for several functions, although these effects hardly occurred simultaneously, the system could shift from one way of operation to another when required.

Trans-structures are however inherently multifunctional systems and take a step further in the same development process. The union of core and medium provides responsiveness, which requires the structure to be a heat mass, heater/cooler and load-bearing system at the same time. Additionally, Trans-structure unites engineering and structural functions in one system.

MULTI-FUNCTIONALITY OF TRANS-STRUCTURE ELIMINATES THE INHERENT COMPROMISES OF ISOLATED CONSTITUENT DESIGN AND THE PROBLEM OF INCREASED EMBEDDED ENERGY DEMAND OF MULTIPLE ELEMENT ASSEMBLY. TRANS-STRUCTURES ARE IN THIS SENSE CONSTRUCTIONS BETWEEN TWO EXTREMES: THE MONOLITHIC ASPECT OF THE VERNACULAR AND THE COMPLEXITY OF THE MODERN INDUSTRIAL.

'Pattern Panel' project is a multifunction prototype experiment, conducted in Kengo Kuma Laboratory at the University of Tokyo. The goal of the research was to design and create building elements with wide variety of functions. Heating and cooling was provided by the water infill, which operated as a fluid medium in the structure. The engineering system included an external heat storage, in which the absorbed heat surplus could be stored for later usage.

Naturally, the water worked as an effective thermal mass and also as insulation, assured by the time-lag effect of the water volume. Because of the increased weight and internal pressure, the fluid infill also served structural purposes together with the solid core. The final and most important property was the change of transparency.

Material test for Pattern Panel Project
© Jenny Kan and Jagoda Krawczyk

When it comes to multifunctionality of Pattern Panel, the interrelations of different functions are essential. Smart materials and kinetic technologies are capable to change transparency of building envelope, but such systems fail to take advantage of the process. Pattern Panel is however a Trans-structure, which means that immediate responses are not only triggered by the effect directly, but the changes are also in proportion with the intensity of the effect itself. Additionally, the change in opacity this case is more than a shading solution, because less transparency also increases absorption of the water volume at the same time. The utilized thermochromic painting on the structure allowed a continuous change of the building envelope in direct relationship to external temperature and insolation.

On a typical hot summer day, the cold water from the external temperature kept the water infill in ideal temperature range and resulting in low opacity. In winter, the process is reversed, the structure warms the interior and hot water increases transparency in order to provide high solar gain for the interior. The building element this way is not only a heater/cooler, perimeter structure or thermal mass, but also absorber and a shading device as well. More importantly, the changes for each function are kept in relation to the other to assure ideal and proportional structural response at all possible effects and climate scenarios.

Prototype test for Pattern Panel Project
© Jenny Kan and Jagoda Krawczyk

PATTERN PANEL IS A NEW
APPROACH TO RESPONSIVE
BUILDING ENVELOPE:

THE CHANGES ARE PROPORTIONAL
AND TRIGGERED INSTANTLY
BY EXTERNAL EFFECTS;
FURTHERMORE, THE SYSTEM
BECOMES CAPABLE TO BENEFIT
FROM THEM WHILE GENERATING
COUNTERMEASURES TO ASSURE
STABILITY OF THE MICROCLIMATE.

In this sense, the project is an attempt to search for possible future developments for architecture and construction methods by taking the requirements of sustainability as sources of inspiration.

1 R. Banham: Architetcure of the Well Tempered Environment, The University of Chicago Press, Chicago, 1969

ENER-GY

CONSUMPTION AND MATTER

ENERGY
CONSUMPTION AND MATTER

Energy demand for building operation is crucial for sustainable architecture. When it comes to 'passive' or 'active' housing, the goal is clearly to minimize the energy impact of a project by lowering energy demand for thermal comfort. The standards for passive house for example, define limitations for heating-cooling and primary energy consumption. In addition to energy concerns, air tightness of building envelope is a crucial factor as well. Passive house can however effectively lower energy demand for building operation, but this does not come without a price. Superinsulation, required for such structure covering the whole building envelope with 335 mm thick insulation for walls and 500 mm for roofs (13 in, 0.1 W/m2K and 20 in, 0066 W/m2K respectively). Besides building cost, this increases material need for building envelope considerably. Passive house therefore seems to be at odds with sustainability today: in order to achieve low primary energy, we are forced to spend more on materials; and total life cycle energy impact of any project therefore grows much higher than initially expected, mainly because of two reasons.

Firstly, building envelopes' embedded energy
became considerably higher compared to
the past, not only because new technologies
or materials, but also because of stricter
energy standards of construction; following
sustainability and energy conservation agendas.
Diagrams shows the development for building
technology from 10 thousand BC until today.
The thickness of each curve shows the energy
demand of the particular material and the length
represents the historical period when it was
used as a primary material for construction.
Naturally, some materials, like stone serves
as building material since the dawn of known
history, without much significant change of
construction or energy demand as it can be
seen in the diagram as well. The embedded
energy need of some materials that appear later,
decreases when manufacture processing and
technology develops or recycling is introduced. This
is typical for glass, steel or aluminum as expected.

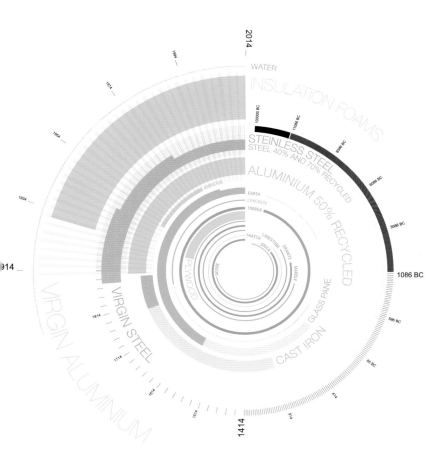

*Embodied Energy of
building materials in history*

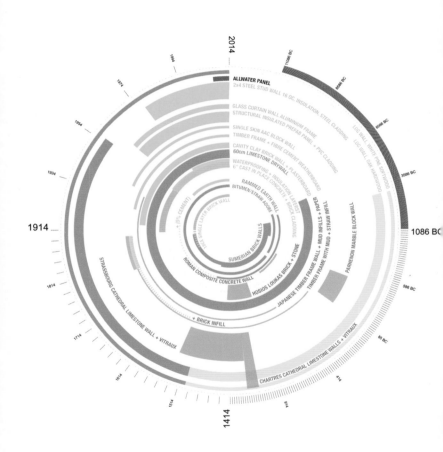

*Embodied Energy of
perimeter structures in history*

However, what is perhaps most important here is the embedded energy demand of insulation: which requires significant energy need compared with any other material. More importantly, the necessary volume for perimeter structures is increasing constantly at the same time. While primary structural members require less material with the advancement of engineering and technology, the thickness of insulation in buildings increased in the last decades. This is why today, when it comes to life cycle energy bill, the demand of building material sector becomes more important part of the total energy impact, while in the past decades operating energy still represented 90-95% of the total share. [1,2]

The second important aspect is life expectancy of our buildings today. Although elements of perimeter structure vary from 28-30 to even 86 years, our buildings rarely manage to last that long. This is a crucial factor, because the energy initially embodied in a building can be as much as 67% of its operating energy over a 25 years period. Naturally, with lower lifespan the significance of embodied energy increases further. This is crucial even for timber construction, since the life cycle is inherently lower; therefore, the proportion of embodied energy increases even further.

This contradiction is however difficult to solve, since for thermal comfort requirement, mass and insulation are both required. When it comes to conventional structures and construction methods, this limitation remains inevitable. Regardless of expected development in technology, the increase of embodied energy remains an essential factor and the basic correlation remains: operational energy cannot be lowered without more mass if the model remains the same.

IN ORDER TO ACHIEVE SIGNIFICANT SAVINGS FOR BOTH, THE MODEL ITSELF HAS TO BE RECONSIDERED AND RECONFIGURED.

AGAIN, THE PROBLEM IS WITH THE MODEL AND NOT WITH THE STRUCTURE.

Trans-structure is based on effective energy distribution and exchange, and this way it is capable to assure the same quality of thermal comfort with less operational and embodied energy simultanously. As explained in the previous chapter, both hybrid and fusion models can incorporate large thermal mass without embodied energy investment while in the same time minimizing the total energy impact. 'Allwater Panel', a hybrid trans-structure can achieve the same indoor requirements with significant energy savings with lower embodied energy than conventional structures. This is acheived through alternative material use and the energy model. By effective energy storage and absorption, insulation is not necessary to achieve low energy standards, and furthermore, water is available without energy investment which makes it ideal building material and also perfect solution for long-term energy storage or distribution.

[1] A. Hallquist: Energy consumption: manufacture of building materials and building construction, Habitat Intlernational, 3 (5/6) (1978), pp. 551–557

[2] B. Hannon, R.G. Stein, B.Z. Segal, D. Serber: Energy and labor in the construction sector, Science, 202 (24/11/78) (1978), pp. 837–847

[3] Y.G. Yohanis, B. Norton: Life-cycle operational and embodied energy for a generic single-storey office building in the UK, Energy
Volume 27, Issue 1, January 2002, Pages 77–92

———————————————

As the examples in the next chapters will show, trans-structure is therefore not only a new method for environment friendly building with low operational energy, but also an important step towards a low embodied energy sustainable construction.

TWO

TOWARDS TRANS-STRUCTURES

MEMU MEADOWS

Living room with the central fireplace
© Kengo Kuma and Associates

TRADITION AND INNOVATION

Interview with *Mr. Takuma Saikawa*,
Project Architect of *Même, Kengo Kuma Architects and Associates*

Tokyo, 14th February 2014

The experimental house of Même located in Northern Japan may only be a small building among the impressive number of projects of Kengo Kuma and Associates, yet an important one in many ways. The project is deeply rooted in the history and conditions of the site, so it creates well-tempered environment with new approach to thermal comfort. These qualities not only make this project unique, but are also truly rare in Japanese architecture. On February 14th 2014, we spoke to Mr. Takumi Saikawa, the project architect of Même in KKAA Tokyo office, about his experience and inspirations.

Matyas Gutai: Thinking about Memu Meadows house in Hokkaido, one inevitably interlinks tradition with innovation. For start, can you please tell us about the sources of inspiration for this project?

Takumi Saikawa: Our office has a unique design philosophy for architecture that we always follow, but we normally start with research about history of the place. We need to think about the site, what sort of impression, in terms of atmosphere and ambience, one perceives while visiting it. Human scale and history is very important to us. In case of Memu Meadows at first we looked into the traditional architecture of Hokkaido and found Ainu residence "Chise". I believe the main reason why Kuma-san was originally interested in this model is because he studied vernacular architecture in the laboratory of Hiroshi Hara.

MG: What was the main goal of focus you pursued in this particular project? Was it related to new architecture, new lifestyle or new type of energy system?

TS: Every project has its own aim and own goal, and the focus depends on particular case. We always try to think of new possibilities in architecture and about the future of our lives. In Japan many companies specialize for housing construction, but for most of them a house is simply just a product to sell. Architecture becomes overly commercialized. However, in Kengo Kuma and Associates, we always search for new possibilities of life style. These investigations may take shape in a new energy system, new façade structure or a new spatial composition of program.

Living room in the morning
© Kengo Kuma and Associates

MG: When you visited the site, what was your main source of inspiration?

TS: In our office site and history (traditions) are very important. When I visit the site, I try to imagine the interior of the building that will emerge in that place. In case of Même, location and good visual connection with nature was important for the design.

Window positions were defined by these views, looking from inside the house towards nature. Bedroom window height, for example, is adjusted according to the beds, and position and dimension of the living room openings take the height of people seating on tatami mat into account. The spatial experience defined by that was very important for us.

MG: Can you please explain how the building works? The energy system of Même seems to be essential for the whole design concept.
TS: We first researched traditional architecture of "Chise", the original dwelling for Ainu people. They had a unique heating system with a central fireplace which also utilizes the surrounding soil as thermal mass. The most important quality of this model was, that it takes advantage of the ground's heat, and by that also maintains a Japanese lifestyle which is traditionally very much more connected to tatami mat and being seated on the floor. But these buildings are not warm enough for contemporary life standards. To achieve the same quality of lifestyle and use of soil mass, we installed hot water pipes in the foundation. 'Architecture close to the ground', as Kuma-san defined it was crucial for this project.

Additionally, compared to a traditional "Chise" house, we had to rethink material use since vernacular structures could not offer sufficient insulation. Another problem was illumination. Climate is colder in Northern Japan and window sizes are much more restrained than in Tokyo which makes the interiors darker. Normally the solution would be to make a thicker wall to assure good indoor climate, but instead of that we designed a translucent wall for more light. Although insulation this way became lower, this does not affect thermal comfort because we installed hot water pipes also in the wall.

Bedroom
© Kengo Kuma and Associates

The wall consists of an inner and outer layer: the external is translucent insulation, and the internal is a void in which the warm air can circulate. The combination of heat pipe system with the insulation could maintain good indoor environment even with low water temperatures because the radiating surface became very high. I believe this was the most important discovery.

MG: The translucent wall is basically opposite of Chise but the foundation is traditional. You basically separated the building into two parts.

TS: Yes, because heating system was still good for us but the building envelope was not adjustable for our current lifestyle. We basically developed the Chise concept, and shifted to a new typology and building system.

MG: The energy model basically allows a very light building with all the benefits of a heavy structure because the connection to the earth. The foundation stores energy and when interior would get colder it simply reheats it.

TS: The central fireplace and additional electric heating system are utilized to produce hot water. The hot water tubes transfer the heat to the floor and walls. The concrete foundation is directly connected to the ground to store more heat. In the walls, tubes are located in the bottom part and warming the air inside which flows upwards to the roof automatically. This increases the total area of warm radiating surfaces around us which provide ideal thermal comfort. Since the building is located in Hokkaido, cooling was not an issue for the design; we only had to concentrate on the heating during the winter.

"IT IS A NATURAL
AND MILD
VENTILATION
SYSTEM, VERY
EFFECTIVE DURING
WINTER AND
SUMMER AS WELL"

Detail of the interior textile wall surface
© Kengo Kuma and Associates

Living room in the evening
© Kengo Kuma and Associates

MG: Energy model and lifestyle seems crucial for this building, and the innovation is directly connected to the building tradition of the area. Were there any other sources of inspiration?
TS: I think Même derives directly from Chise. We developed it only further with new building technologies available to us today.

MG: We are dealing with novel material use and energy model, resulting an innovative architecture rooting in tradition. Which were the most important from these 3 aspects?
TS: This is a very difficult question, since architecture is related to many problems. Energy is one problem and material is another, but so is structure, engineering, economy, history and culture for example. Problems and solutions are changing all the time. In these last 10 or 20 years, we have to think of energy or economy systems, especially after Tohoku earthquake. However, the buildings will be used for a longer time, and after 50 years or 100 years, the focus will change again. Actual and recent problems are of course important, but we always need to think about the future and its relation to the historical context as well. In case of Même project, the energy system and lifestyle pays attention to the traditions of the area, but also attempts to define a new concept which I hope will contribute to development of architecture in the future.

MG: How do you see the future of this architectural approach?

TS: In Hokkaido the houses are normally very closed. Windows are very small, interiors filled with relatively less sunlight, and energy demand is substantial. I hope Même will present a completely new solution for cold climates like Hokkaido in the future.

MG: Would you say that this energy model and system could create new possibilities in architecture?

TS: Yes, this kind of energy model gives us new paradigm in design since it allows us to think of translucentstructures, or translucent perimeter structures even in cold climate of Hokkaido, and not only in warm areas like Okinawa for example.

MG: Would you say that this also defines new lifestyle? When I was staying in the building, I was truly impressed by the quality of thermal comfort indoors, so rare in Japan, as well as the effect of translucent envelope. I literally woke up with the Sun.

TS: Yes, I believe such architecture has the possibility to change the lifestyle of the people. We need to feel closer to the nature through architecture even when we are in a big city like Tokyo or Sapporo. I think this project has some potential for that.

I stayed a few times in Même. Without heating system constantly operating, we can feel temperature of sunlight. It was very interesting experience for me. After a normal day, the heating system can be turned off and the house relies on thermal mass to keep the building comfortable and warm. In Japan it is very new experience because normally we use active systems exclusively, like air-conditioner.

MG: How do you see this affecting the future? Can such design approach divert the work of KKAA to some new directions?

TS: Architecture has many possibilities for adopting the human life. Lixil Foundation (the Client for Même) organizes student competition on this topic every year. Last year we worked together with the students of Harvard GSD on the Horizon house project, which won the 1st Prize. The building will be built next to Même house. I am personally very interested in energy systems of architecture and I would like to continue working on more energy-efficient and ecological architecture. The research on this façade system continues, and we are recently did a factory project with the same translucent façade system.

The building in the evening
© Kengo Kuma and Associates

THIS EXPERIMENTAL HOUSE IN THE ADVERSE CLIMATE OF NORTHERN JAPAN IS A UNIQUE FUSION OF LOCAL VERNACULAR ARCHITECTURAL KNOWLEDGE WITH CONTEMPORARY DESIGN AND LATEST BUILDING TECHNOLOGIES.

ARCHAIC TO CONTEMPORARY

Memu-Meadows house

The collaboration of Kengo Kuma and Associates with the Institute of Industrial Design at the University of Tokyo made this new building type possible which takes advantage of the Chise model of Ainu architecture, integrating it with new building materials and structural system. The result is a reinterpretation of the archaic buildings which has not only effect on thermal comfort but also drives the design and creates extraordinary atmosphere.

The traditional house of Chise utilizes the thermal mass of the ground below the building; the central fireplace is also sunken below the floor to increase the heat storage effect. Memu Meadows takes a further step on this path: in addition to the central fireplace and soil storage, the walls and roof became even lighter, and all perimeter surfaces are united by an air layer embedded in the structure.

The air layer becomes the medium of the trans-structure which carries heat from one location to another when necessary, distributing the heat coming from the ground, and finally it stores heat in the increased air layer of the roof structure.

This innovative solution is also combined with a translucent insulation so the house remains strongly connected to its surroundings in sense of both energy and natural light. The house and the interior opens up when the sunlight enters in the morning through the translucent skin and gradually turns into itself by the end of the day. In this manner, the house reconnects us with nature and aims for a new lifestyle and architecture at the same time.

HEATING CYCLE

STORAGE CYCLE

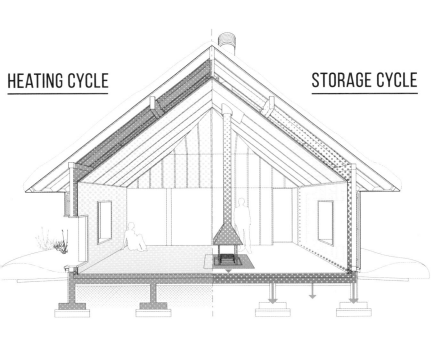

*Section and energy diagram
in heating and storage cycles*

WATER
BRANCH

HYBRID BUILDING

Interview with **Ms. Tomoko Sasaki**,
Architect of ***Water Block project of Kengo Kuma and Associates***

Tokyo, 30th May 2014

Water Branch is a unique project in which engineering and technology is united in one hybrid structure. The research took years until Kuma Laboratory built the first house for Gallery MA exhibition (project leader Mr. Nishikawa). Ms. Sasaki of Kengo Kuma and Associates worked with Mr. Miyazawa and Mr. Ohba one stage before that, when during the MOMA exhibition the project became a real structure. On May 30th, with my colleague Yuta Ito, we asked her about the project in KKAA Tokyo office.

Matyas Gutai: First of all, I would like to ask you about the inspiration for this project, since introducing plastic and water as structural material is rather unique. Can you please explain in detail how the idea came up and how it developed into a real structure?

Tomoko Sasaki: Originally it started with a water block which was a plastic tank with 2 cylinders on top. The blocks were designed to interlock with each other to make a wall. The first project was exhibited in Milano Salon. After that we proposed the same idea for a competition organized by MoMA on temporary housing. The plastic units first served as containers to send food and water to disaster areas. After reaching its destination, the plastic units could be used as building blocks. The proposal was a success, and we could exhibit the concept in MoMA. The structure was only ideal for stacking that stage, and we were not thinking to use it for roof stucture for example. A fabric cover served that purpose.

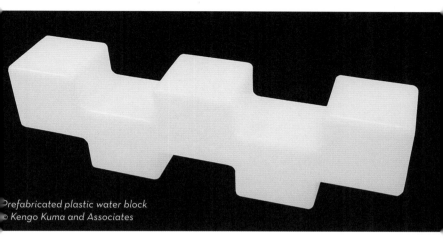

Prefabricated plastic water block
© Kengo Kuma and Associates

Fortunately we had time and opportunity to develop the system further before the installation. We modified the block so we became able to also make roof and beams with it. We studied possibilities of longer element types, as well as concave and convex forms (in Japanese letters: 凹 and 凸). The final unit had the shape of both in the end, and could not only be stacked up, but also could be used to build a frame structure.

The Water Branch house built for Gallery-Ma exhibition in Tokyo came one year later in 2009.

In the MOMA exhibition, we only exhibited walls and floors because of budget restrictions. However, we designed a load-bearing frame structure that can be developed from our concept. In case of Gallery MA exhibition, the block was used for building a roof as well.

MG: Can you please explain how the idea came up originally? Does it trace back to another building, a traditional element or perhaps nature?

TS: In the beginning of Water Block project Kuma-san used the example of plastic tanks filled with water and used as barricades mainly in construction sites. The idea of a stacked and filled block came from there, similar to LEGO joints. In the Water Branch project, we developed it further and looked for possible assembly methods, but the results became too complicated. We decided to modify length and shape instead to make sequentially joined blocks, and finally came up with a joint system similar to Japanese wooden joints.

Exhibition at MOMA, New York
© *Kengo Kuma and Associates*

Exhibition at Gallery MA, Tokyo
© Kengo Kuma and Associates

MG: The house exhibited in Gallery-Ma also differed from the earlier solutions in inbuilt heating-cooling system. Could you explain the main differences?

TS: MoMA's project started from the idea of temporal housing that shelters people. The focus was on the joint system that time, although we proposed the possibility of wiring-like equipment. However, in case of Gallery-Ma exhibition, we developed it to a futuristic, contemporary housing concept with necessary equipment for longer use.

In fact, in the beginning we just wanted to store drinking water (important for disaster areas) and make beams. During the MOMA exhibition project, we noticed that sequential connection has other advantages. We recognized that we can also create water pipes and the blocks can store water at the same time. This way the blocks became insulation material or heat storage.

The idea came from the structure, but we explored and added new properties in a way: structural and thermal mass, food storage, and also new environmental technologies like heating or electricity production.

MG: Can you please emphasize the most important advantages and challenges of such structure?

TS: The basic block is small and light, and therefore building is easy and simple. The system is recyclable and also reusable. The small unit can later on be used for another building with different shape. The element's size gives us real flexibility. The most important challenge may be its current limitation. At this stage it cannot be used to build larger structures.

MG: Can you please tell us about the future possibilities of this technology? Is the research on Water House in its final stage or can we expect more projects to come? What could be the new ways for development?

TS: There are several possibilities. We can revise the joint to make the structure stronger, or we can develop it to a façade system with embedded environmental equipment. But the main question is the scale of the block itself, because larger buildings will require a bigger unit. Our block was determined by the original design of a temporary shelter. We wanted maximum 5 kg weight for easy assembly and the size was also limited by rotation fabrication process.

Plastic mold for the water block
© Kengo Kuma and Associates

MG: Have you also considered combining your block with conventional load-bearing frame?
TS: The main idea in our office was always to develop this block to a structural system. In addition to wall, we were always thinking to build columns, beams or roof structures with it as well.

Takumi Saikawa: I think in this system the size of the module and multi-functionality of the building element is essential. Kuma-san was thinking about system, block and structure at the same time. The design was never limited to the block itself, nevertheless it focused on structure and also on engineering equipment. He was thinking of a multifunctional element from the beginning. I believe we need further structural studies if we aim for a larger building, like a house project in the future, but the main concept of multifunctional blocks will remain.

MG: Perhaps the multifunctionality is the most important and progressive aspect of this concept since our conventional building practice is typically mono-functional.
TS: Thank you.

MG: Thank you very much for the interview.

Construction of Water Branch House
in Gallery MA, Tokyo
© Kengo Kuma and Associates

WATER-BRANCH NOT ONLY DEFINED A TRANS-STRUCTURE SYSTEM BY INTEGRATING WATER AND PLASTIC SHELL, BUT ALSO WAS CAPABLE TO BENEFIT FROM THE POTENTIAL OF THE NEW STRUCTURAL SYSTEM TO DEFINE A NEW LIFESTYLE AND SPATIAL ATMOSPHERE.

STREAM CONSTRUCTION
Water Branch House

The plastic brick assured easy assembly and reuse; the water provided an accessible thermal mass and insulation for ideal indoor comfort. The idea was later developed to Water-branch project and exhibited in MOMA New York. Finally, a temporary house was built in Gallery MA Tokyo, for 'Kengo Kuma: Studies in Organic' exhibition. The plastic-water bricks have not provided only the structure of the house, but also heating/cooling and insulation for the space.

The bricks were connected to each other and formed a stream which flows from floor through the wall up to the roof of the building. Connected to geothermal heating and cooling, and available almost at any location in Japan, the structure formed an ideal fusion of lightweight structural core and water medium with limited capacity of trans-structure: responses to environmental condition by utilizing external energy sources.

External effects were primarily counteracted by the considerable thermal mass capacity. In case that proved to be insufficient, geothermal energy covered the additional demand.

This solution was not only important for the energy concept of the project, the final goal was to define a self-sufficient housing system which is capable to aim for a different lifestyle in Japanese archipelago which is currently dependent to Tokyo and its centralized services. In this manner, Water-branch not only defined a trans-structure system by integrating water and plastic shell, but also was capable to benefit from the potential of the new structural system to define a new lifestyle and spatial atmosphere.

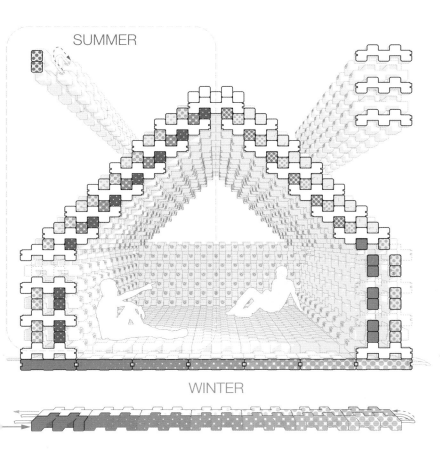

SUMMER

WINTER

*Section and energy diagram in
summer and winter*

HYGRO SKIN
PAVILION

HygroScope detail © ICD University of Stuttgart

INMADE SMARTNESS

Interview with *Prof. Achim Menges*,
Professor at *Institute for Computational Design of University of Stuttgart*

Stuttgart, 15th May 2014

Prof. Achim Menges and his team at Institute for Computational Design of University of Stuttgart... worked for 7 years before the first pavilion with embedded material responsiveness was built. The structure and design methodology behind it is neither pure biomimicry nor a high-tech environmental system: it is rather both, a search for a new paradigm in sustainable design and construction.

Matyas Gutai: Your research focuses on morphogenetic and computational design. Embedded material responsiveness becomes important part of your work a bit later.

Prof. Achim Menges: Our interest in passively responsive materials stems from our research in material systems and their relation to computation. Computational processes are one of the drivers of all our work. Computation, the way we think of it, relates to both digital as well as physical processes.

In this way, the computer can be 'instrumentalized' to understand and explore physical processes that usually are beyond the designer's sense and intuition, and to think about possible syntheses of form, structure and material performance. Developing such computational processes has been an overall interest for 12 years by now which eventually resulted in the recognition that materials are not simply an inner matter and that there are even materials that demonstrate very particular behaviors in exchange with the environment. Of course, all materials arguably are effected by environmental conditions, but there are some that do this in a very pronounced manner. For example, wood occurred to us as particularly interesting because arguably it is one of the oldest building materials. Its something that always sits in a kind of ecological relation with the environment. That is because wood is a hygroscopic material which means that it desorbs and absorbs water molecules from the atmosphere. The tricky thing is that this exchange with the surrounding environment on a molecular level actually leads to changes in the material properties.

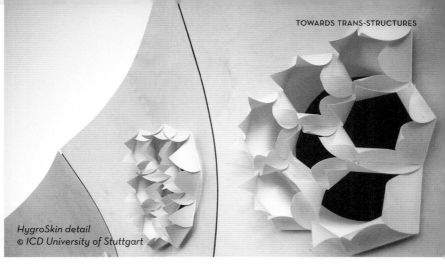

HygroSkin detail
© ICD University of Stuttgart

So on the one hand, an intake of water molecules reduces the stiffness of the material, and on the other hand it triggers a dimensional change. Because of its cellular structure the resultant material behavior is anisotropic, leading to a differential length change in a sense, wood fulfills all the expected characteristics of so called smart building materials: it adapts to its environment and this response results in a change of shape and mechanical properties. So it really is a very versatile and effective building material with a highly sophisticated internal structure. However, in today's construction industry, it is usually conceived merely as a kind of geometric entity. Probably most emblematic for this are the US naming conventions for timber which is not even called wood but just 2x2 or 4x4 and so on. In contrast, we were interested in working with wood's intricate anatomy and characteristics by really exploiting the material's innate behavior of weather responsiveness. Rather than understanding the dimensional instability of wood as a deficiency (as in the history of architecture and craft that spans for about 3-4 thousand years, which always tried to suppress this innate behavior), we started to investigate how we can 'instrumentalise' it.

Hygroscopic behavior of spruce cones
© ICD University of Stuttgart

We figured out that there are actually natural systems that do exactly this. Most emblematic are so called plant cones which utilize the differential length change of woody materials – actually lining cellulose composites – to achieve a shape change. There are many passively actuated plant movements that act in a very similar manner, but spruce cones are an interesting example because they are dead plant organs. They fall of the tree and once they change shape in response to environmental conditions they are no longer connected to the plants metabolism so it doesn't depend on energy that is actually fed through the plant system. This is obviously very different to actively actuated moves of the leaves of mimosa which are triggered by cell pressure changes. Cone movement is entirely passive and it just operates in the most reliable and robust fashion. Based on these principles, in the last 7 years we developed passively hygroscopic systems that use the actual "intelligence" of wood as a responsive layer of an adaptive veneer-composite element.

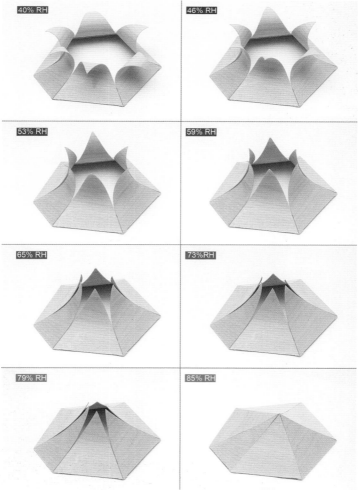

HygroSkin opening in changing humidity © ICD University of Stuttgart

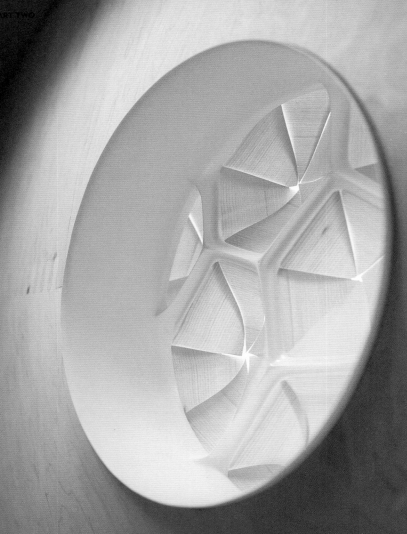

MG: Do you mean composite system in sense of different material uses or layers of the same wood in different grain angle?

AM: In this case both. We experimented with wood as a natural composite, 'instrumentalising' the possibility of varying grain directions of the wood and by that achieving the similar bi-layer effect that ultimately enables the movement. But we also experimented quite a bit with synthetic composite materials that have a lot of advantages when it comes to stabilizing the reactive layer adding rigidity, longevity, reliability, particularly when it comes to long durations of inactiveness. Wood creeps and the cellular structure adapts to a particular shape and that is sort of counterbalanced by the synthetic composite. Another issue is that the thin layers of wood are not particularly UV resistant and the composite also provides protection against that.

But what I really like to stretch is that the composite is playing the 'dumb role' and the smart bit is wood. It is perfectly possible just to laminate the same structure only using wood by compromising the longevity.

MG: You have mentioned 7 years of research. Can you please tell us a few words about the main steps of the work until the point of construction of the pavilion?

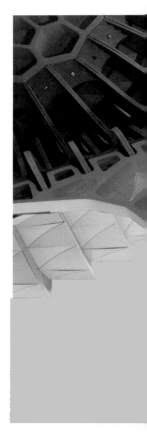

AM: Over these 7 years we have done a whole number of mock-ups and tests. It really started when I took a professorship in Offenbach at the school of art and industrial design. It was very interesting to work with the designers there, as they have more immediate relationship with material and process of materialization. There was one particularly talented and outstanding student, Steffen Reichert, who you may know as co-author of all related publications. At my department he did a pre-diploma project on a responsive system which we subsequently called "Responsive Surface Structure 1".

This still relied on a kind of substructure but exhibited already the capacity of adapting to humidity changes. He has continued that in his diploma project with a number of innovative aspects, some of them conceptually still advanced and we are still trying to implement them.

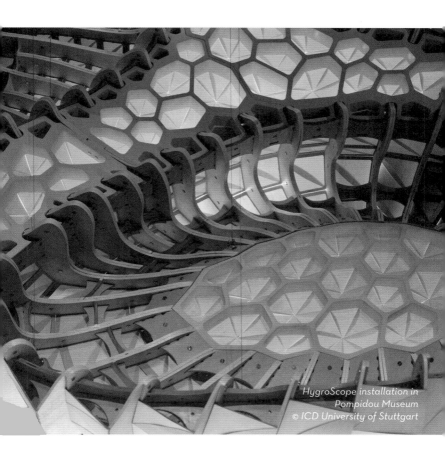

HygroScope installation in Pompidou Museum
© ICD University of Stuttgart

He had a kind of continuous transition from reactive panels to actual structural panels and the same material would have a responsive tip and a structural end. By that time we started to develop the computational tools also. Steffen went away to study at the MIT for 2 years and at the same time I went to Stuttgart where we did a whole number of feasibility studies and set up a long-term test at our rooftop for almost 3 years. We did a lot of catching up with the technicalities and underlying principles during that period and when Steffen came back from the MIT we had a chance to really push the research considerably as we were commissioned to develop an installation for the permanent collection of the Centre Pompidou in Paris which is the "HygroScope – Metereosensitive Morphology" installation. In Pompidou it resides in a glass box in which we simulate the outside climate of Paris and you can actually see the motion of the 'meterosensitive' morphology and visually perceive the changes of relative humidity that human sensory system are usually not very sensitive for. The concept behind that installation was to show how responsive a building material can be and also present how dynamic our environment is by putting that wooden installation into the glass case which sits in arguably one of the most stable climate in the world - the interior of the Pompidou museum.

Open and Closed HygroScope © ICD University of Stuttgart

This project led to the commission of the HygroSkin pavilion for the FRAC Centre which was simply thrilling, because it really allowed us to speculate on what would be a building skin that takes advantage of this performative system and what kind of effect would that produce both thermodynamically but also architecturally. It turned out to be a unique convergence of spatial and environmental experiences that are really weather dependent and again take advantage of this very simple system of responsive actuation. It is also interesting to note that, in Pompidou, we worked exactly in the opposite way than in the FRAC pavilion. In the first case, the system actually opens with an increase in relative humidity while in the pavilion it is closing. This was possible because in those 7 years we did quite a lot of studies on how we can physically program the behavior of the material. We can actually have exactly the same material, same structure and ingredient, and still we are in the position to develop a fabrication process which programs the material to behave in exactly opposite manner.

MG: Comparing an artistic installation with a building there are obviously different demands and goals. Can you please explain how the building 'behaves' - if I can use that term?

AM: The HygroSkin pavilion's skin is basically in ecological relation with the immediate surroundings. The wood-veneer composite is at the same time the sensor, the motor and the regulating element. We like to use the phrase that here "the material is the machine".

The apertures respond to relative humidity changes within a range from 30% to 90%, which equals the humidity range from bright sunny to rainy weather in a moderate climate. In direct feedback with the local microclimate, the pavilion constantly adjusts its degree of openness and porosity, modulating the light transmission and visual permeability of the envelope. This exchange results in constant fluctuations of enclosure, illumination, and interiority of the internal space. The hygroscopic actuation of the surface provides for a unique convergence of environmental and spatial experience; the perception of the delicate, locally varied, and ever changing environmental dynamics is intensified through the subtle and silent movement of the 'meteorosensitive' architectural skin.

The changing surface embodies the capacity to sense, actuate, and react, all within the material itself.

In the longer-term perspective, I don't actually conceive this as a façade system of a fully indoor space. We rather see it as an autonomously responsive skin for semi-outdoor spaces.

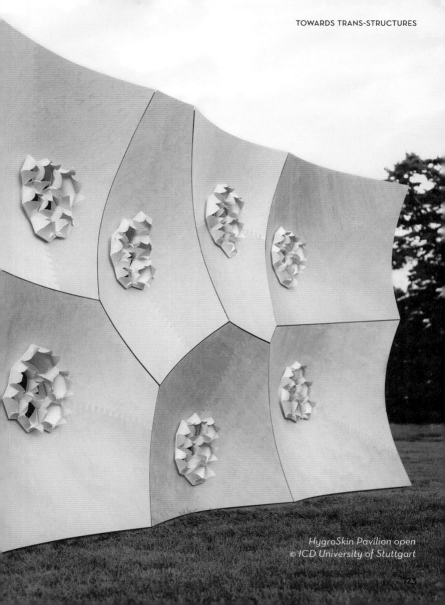

HygroSkin Pavilion open
© ICD University of Stuttgart

A very good example would be a football stadium roof with its requirement for opening in order to allow the grass to grow. Some of the most daring and complex structures are big stadium roofs like the Wembley stadium with huge metal plates that slide up and down. We thought - why don't we use design strategies that nature employs to assure small movement and autonomous responses: a stadium roof that is open all the time and in case of rain it actually closes and operates in a kind of binary manner. Passive systems have no user override which is always a challenge. That's why I think it is much more suitable situation to use them when there is a binary relation with the requirement.

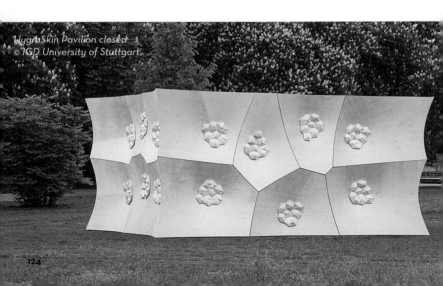

HygroSkin Pavilion closed
© ICD University of Stuttgart

MG: We reached the topic of possible future of such implications. You already mentioned examples for implementation but at the same time there is a new design thinking behind it since it leaves predetermined structural state behind in order to build an inherently responsive structural system.

AM: What I find very interesting is that these systems challenge our preconceptions about materials and the design of materials. One question I asked myself quite often is that the materials we used in HygroScope and HygroSkin have been around for a long time, the technologies we use are also fully accessible, why only now do we actually come up with these systems? There is not any kind of technological bottleneck that would have prevented this development 20 years ago. I think the key innovation is the design thinking! We began to have really a different look at materials. We also have a different way of conceiving of fabrication and materialization processes. I think that we are moving away from an understanding that design means the superimposition of form on an inert matter.

What we are trying to do generally is to have the materials to play a much more active role in design processes. Today we are even able to extend the behavior of material into the lifespan of the actual structure. I think this is really a new paradigm of design which first and foremost proves to be an intellectual challenge for the designer. Only now we are beginning to have a conceptualization of design which allows us to actually work in this manner. This is for me one of the crucial aspects. Additionally, we have good reasons to investigate similar "design principles" for material-innate behavior - as the passive actuation we discussed above - in different fields, such as biology, but also for example vernacular architecture . I think there is occasionally a really striking similarity between the culturally evolved vernacular architecture and biologically evolved natural systems in regards to employing and utilizing material capacities. In terms of biology, we are beginning to be in position to actually tap into that enormous reservoir of possibilities that living nature offers because of the advances in computational design, simulation, and fabrication.

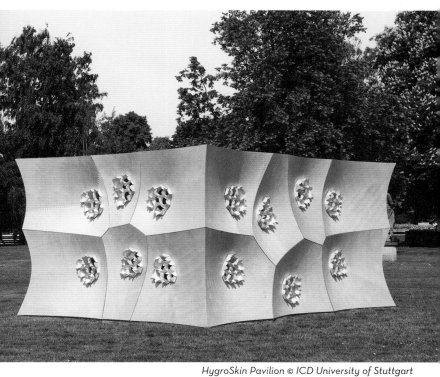

HygroSkin Pavilion © ICD University of Stuttgart

HYGROSKIN AND THE RESEARCH WORK OF PROF. ACHIM MENGES IS AN EXCELLENT EXAMPLE OF HOW A CHALLENGE CAN BE TURNED INTO ADVANTAGE INSTEAD OF WORKING AGAINST IT.

EMBEDDED RESPONSIVENESS
HygroSkin Pavilion

The inspiration for the project comes from biology: the hygroscopic behavior was taken as the model to develop a response-able perimeter skin for buildings.

Conifer cones change shape depending on moisture and this property was used to develop a building skin which can control ventilation and shading in interior space. With changes in humidity, the thin wooden layers of surface openings gradually get adapted as well. This solution has various advantages at the same time: changes occur gradually without additional control, monitoring, or energy demand since the external effects modify the skin directly. This also makes the responses proportional to the changes in the environment.

After several prototypes and temporary
constructions, the research on HygroSkin
recently built the first pavilion in Stuttgart and
now develops change-able construction elements
and systems for projects on a larger scale.

HygroSkin project represents a trans-structure
which not only embraces change but also takes
advantage of it. The trans-structure crated by
responsive perimeter skin is an effective tool
of embedded responsiveness, and it is also
an element that redefines architectural space
from static and homogenous experience into a
dynamic spatial atmosphere.

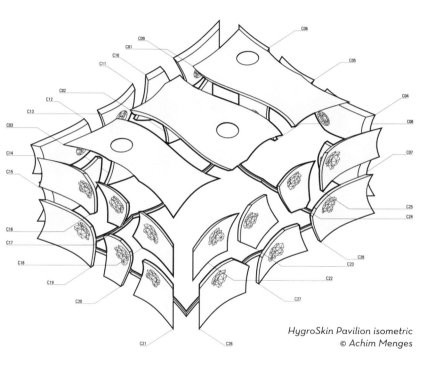

HygroSkin Pavilion isometric
© Achim Menges

BIQ
BUILDING
HAMBURG

BIQ façade panel detail
© Colt, Arup, SSC

STRUCTURE HARVEST

Interview with *Jan Wurm* and *Martin Pauli,*
Associate Director and Architect of *Arup*,
materials consulting

Berlin, 17th July 2014

*Designers Jan Wurm and Martin Pauli of Arup teamed up
with architects SPLITTERWERK , innovators of SSC and
Colt to build the first bioreactor façade. With the support of
Zukunft Bau foundation, they were able to develop the panel
system into a holistic structural element. In Arup´s Berlin
office I asked them about the new design thinking behind this
innovation and about the possible developments in the future.*

Matyas Gutai: In the beginning it is important to understand the background of this unique project. What were the main ideas and inspiration?

Jan Wurm: The project started in 2009 with an international design competition on smart material houses for the international building exhibition IBA in Hamburg. A couple of design teams were invited including SPLITTERWERK. They selected a number of consultants asking support in material façades and building physics and opened up the design process to the whole team. At that point we already had topics we were interested in. My background is in architecture but I have specialized in the design of glass structures. I carried out a research during the 90s, when there was an extreme push on maximizing transparency in the façade. The technical concept of transparency did not really follow the time, looking for a more environmental approach to design building envelopes.

BIQ housing
© Colt, Arup, SSC

Part of our research was a system we called tetrahedronglass with polyhedral volumetric elements that we could array on flat or curved surfaces. The volume of those elements were able to absorb energy and had an environmental potential with aesthetic impact moving away from transparency to a reflective multifaceted appearance. Also, our ex-chairman, Peter Head, started to communicate the potential of algae systems within carbon-cycles and, in a lecture called the Ecological Age, all these systems have been presented in 2008. These were sort of starting points for us.

We first discussed tubular reactors but there were no systems available and also they did not serve an integrated architectural function and did not really lead us towards a full building integration. Mr. Kerner, a manager of a company in Hamburg called Strategic Science Consult or SSC, had a research project going on in 2007-2008 and he had developed a flat panel bioreactor. These are 2-dimensional panels similar to other panel products in the market. However, his system integrated a special geometry for the air uplift that lead to a quite high production rate of biomass, approximately 10 times higher than tubular reactors. They absorb daylight for the photosynthetic process but also cause the medium to heat up. Obviously, when you are over certain threshold, 38 degrees, the algae starts to get stressed and, if it goes to even higher values, they will die. There was a constant need for cooling down the system and doing that in an open-air site is just a mere loss.

The original idea was a house in house concept: the external skin was fitted with photovoltaic on top and with bioreactors on the façade. It was called the Energy Skin. Between the external skin and the actual building there was the zone that the architect called the "Supernature": a mezzo-climate which was not conditioned something between inside and outside. The competition was selected to be one of the winners with direct emphasis to explore the idea of the biofaçade further.

To actually build the project, there was some money available from the International Building Exhibition which was covering basically innovative ideas. There was a trade fair and the idea was to meet with private investors but as a study on a product was still missing, Arup decided to create a consortium to develop it. We took SSC in and also we could win Colt which is a specialist in secondary façade systems. Finally, the Zukunft Bau of the German Government made grant for two years project in 2010. After that we got private investor Otto Wulff on board. But because there was a risk that the product design may not be finished in two years, we had to design it as a secondary system so in case it fails there is a possibility to remove it.

Façade detail
© Colt, Arup, SSC

MG: Basically you had to take a step back due to market or investor's demands, but probably you will go back to that in the future somehow?

JW: Absolutely. The product develops taking step by step. The first step was about to demonstrate the technical possibility. The BIQ project was the opportunity to demonstrate that feasibility.

MG: Thinking about BIQ project, can you please explain, in a few words, how the system works?

JW: It is an excellent shading system which comprises a bioreactor so it generates biomass and solar thermal heat. Through the generation of biomass, it absorbs CO_2. This is the functionality of the system which we call SolarLeaf. The key feature is integration in the mechanical systems of the building which is fully developed and tested in the BIQ Building. This means that we extract the heat out of the system to a heat management center where we either increase it further with a heat pump to a level where we can use it further, or we can use it directly to the radiant heating. If there is no heat demand, we store it in a geothermal storage under the building for later use.

Martin Pauli: We are currently monitoring the building and trying to understand the user acceptance and energy performance since 2013. What we know is that the performance is quite good, we are gaining heat and harvesting the algae. We are also trying to think about how to use the algae, because the initial idea was to burn it. However there are other possibilities like cosmetic or pharmaceutical industry. I think we are ready for the next step. Now we need to enable more architectural flexibility and enhance the integration of more technical features to achieve a multifunctionality.

―――――――――――

MG: So we are really not talking about just a vertical shading garden but a multifunctional element which has an important role in the energetic and structural behavior of the building.

JW: Absolutely. Of course there is a level of redundancy because the private investment involved demanded that the building is also linked to the district heating system for a safety backup.

The second side of it is the biomass processing. We tested and optimized it and actually we are making more heat than we thought we would. The amount of biomass we harvest is about 15 dry mass per m2 in a day. It's a fair amount but it is not enough for cost-efficient biogas production. There is however a demand for high quality biomass for the food and pharmaceutical industry. There are no value chains set up for that but that is what we are working on, to feed those products into a bigger cycle or in an urban water cycle. The most important benefit we have today, compared to photovoltaics, is that energy can be stored without any loss.

———————————————

MG: Can we say that, in addition of being multifunctional, these elements are also responsive elements of the building skin?

JW: Yes, microalgae as such is responsive and probably that is why we are inspired by it, especially the way nature responds to changing conditions: finding an ideal way to shade or open up, to get light, or even to shut down to protect. The biochemical process responds directly to the conditions of daylight, nutrition, and temperature. These three parameters control algae growth and by externally controlling them you can integrate it into a technical cycle.

———————————————

MG: But on the other hand, it is also directly controlled by external effects?

JW: Absolutely. The fascinating thing is to have nature as a shading element in the building. This of course is well known since we have trees obviously, but they have a yearly cycle. Algae grow 10 times faster and do cell division within seven hours which is also our response time.

MG: This is important because rapid responses are one of the features we are discussing in these interviews.

JW: It would be interesting to work with different organisms in the future which are optimized for certain conditions. That would be another level of adaptivness.

MP: In the beginning we tried to use algae from the Arctic because it has a different comfort zone compared to algae that is used to our environment. It will be important for us because today we technically have to create that comfort zone but with other species with whom you don't have to constantly worry about their comfort zone and that would be definitely an important step in the future.

Oxygen inlet detail © Colt, Arup, SSC

MG: That would be my next question. Can you please tell us a little bit about the possibilities of such technology in the future?

JW: I would pick up the thought from talking about the complexity that you generate by fitting out a singular building with such technology. The biofaçade is a key element to create a link between various mass flows: water, food, heat and carbon. It should be really a part of bigger system that we would see much more as an organism. We are talking about number of buildings and industrial symbiosis. We produce biomass and we need an industry that can utilize it, just as we need CO_2 to create that. By looking on what we do currently we can see that we do not get the full advantage of the system. What would be important in the future is to look at a district including different building typologies with changing heat demand also to integrate urban food production to get the full advantage. That is one side and also another element is the water factor.

MP: Talking about district scale, let's take wastewater for example. Imagine a closed loop cycle in which carbon is absorbed through the growth of algae purifying the water. Moreover, in terms of visual appearance, there is a lot of potential and the next step would be to push it a little further. Photovoltaic panels, for instance, have always been rectangular. Now organic PV-panels enable a design flexibility that should also inspire us in direction of Bioreactive façade. We need to create a toolbox for architects which they can use and play with to create their own ideas to grow algae.

MG: That is really fascinating because if we shift from an isolated building to the scale of an urban block with multiple functions for example, with heat share we can even eliminate the problem of heat storage. That could be a completely different paradigm shift when it comes to urbanism and it would finally put architecture in a position where it is not only consumer of potentials but becomes the one creating it for the city.

JW: Could be like that, couldn't it? Something spreading out from one building could create a holistic system. One example could be data centers with a lot of excess heat. If you combine that with a biofaçade, then the algae we produce could feed fish throughout the year and also the heat we produce could be used to keep that pond on an ideal thermal level. The same excess heat can create green house for vegetable farming, or it could be fed back to district heating for a residential area. Now if you put all these different functions together, one investor would never take over the whole thing. There also must be a new way to generate projects which provide interface between the different stakeholders and organizes interest groups within such an organism. That takes us to the design side of things and not only to architecture and engineering. We are talking about food engineers, data center specialists, and all these are forming a new set of teams which are also changing the way we look at design process.

Façade structure detail
© Colt, Arup, SSC

THE ALGAE CONTENT IN PANELS CHANGES CONSTANTLY DEPENDING ON EXTERNAL CONDITIONS AND IT REPRESENTS THE FIRST INSTANCE WHEN THE STATE OF PERPETUAL CHANGE OF BUILDING SKIN IS ACHIEVED BY BIOLOGICAL PROCESS INSTEAD OF PROPERTIES OF SIMPLE MATTER.

RESPONSIVE INSTINCT

Algae powered bioreactor façade

The important innovation in field of building materials opened new possibilities for energy production on building facades. The structure made by algae embedded in translucent water-plastic perimeter panels both utilizes the absorbed heat and the biomass which is constantly harvested from the panels in order to produce further electric power.

BIQ was the first pilot project among residential buildings built together with bio-façade in Hamburg, Germany. The algae content in panels changes constantly depending on external conditions and it represents the first instance when the state of perpetual change of building skin is achieved by biological process instead of properties of simple matter.

Although, in this case, the bioreactor façade of BIQ project is combined with a conventional perimeter structure, it still works as a trans-structure, however in slightly different manner. Here again, instead of manipulating the interior to provide stability, the external effects are counteracted at the perimeter immediately.

The properties of the façade elements (insulation or absorption capacity) depend on the algae population which increases or drops depending on the environmental conditions. However, this does not only affect biomass production but also the solar absorption which inherently increases heat energy production and insulation capacity at the same time. In this manner, unlike in the other examples, trans-structure not only contains stable indoor microclimate, but is also simply wrapped around it for the same effect.

BIQ panel isometric © Arup

TRANS-STRUCTURES

ALL-WATER

PAVILION

Allwater Pavilion

ALLWATER PAVILION
PERFORMATIVE TRANSPARENCY

Architecture could never truly evade the omnipresence of time, which has been influencing design since the very beginning. Various strategies were developed against weathering for instance: materials were designed with reserves to withstand the forces of time, or in other cases, ageing was simply embraced as an esthetic value. Functional changes were another issue and were typically addressed by Multifunctionality or flexibility of space. Environmental changes inspired kinetic architecture and smart materials.

Architecture has always been affected by the forces of time in numerous ways in the past, but the common strategy was more in favor of erasing the changes rather than embracing the challenge of the inevitable as source for inspiration.

ALLWATER PAVILION IS AN ATTEMPT FOR AN APPROACH BY NOT ONLY ACCEPTING CHANGES IN ENVIRONMENT, BUT ALSO DEFINING THEM AS DRIVING FORCES IN DESIGN.

The trans-structure approach, transforms the past lessons into a new paradigm in design thinking regarding both element of time and sustainability of embedded resilience.

Allwater Pavilion is an experimental structure with area of about 6 m^2/64 sq. foot/. As the first built trans-structure, the building serves mainly for research purposes, to collect more data on the structural and energy performance of a hybrid building system. The building was built using prefabricated panels with insulation and structural core, similar to SIP system / Structure Insulated Panels/. All the elements were prefabricated in factory, which was necessary due to the high accuracy requirement of the panel's water layer. Water volumes are located on the inner surface of each panel and are connected to each other by joint elements, which are designed to allow the water flow between the units, but also seal any panel off the system in case of leaking or structural damage. The panels are either transparent or opaque and are made by steel or glass respectively.

1 opaque roof panel core
2 opaque roof panel water layer
3 opaque wall panel core + water layer
4 cooling intake pipe
5 heating return pipe
6 glass roof panel with water layer
7 cooling return pipe
8 glass panel with water layer

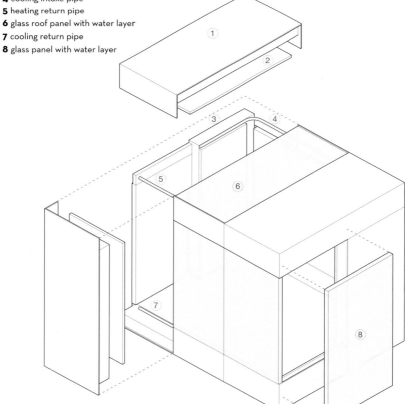

Allwater Pavilion is based on the Water House thermodynamic model recognizing the fact that connected water layers inside a building would be an effective distributor of energy. As a result the water layers assure thermal balance in the whole microclimate regardless of the location or manner of the energy distribution. This model is essential when it comes to embedded responsiveness of the structure.

During cooling periods, the water layers (placed on all internal surfaces) of the structure absorb any heat load indoors. In the beginning, the energy will be stored in the water volume as long as the thermal capacity allows it. Because of effective distribution, the whole structure reacts for any local load; therefore, the thermal storage is significantly higher than for a solid structure, since any local heat gain will be balanced coherently with the capacity of the whole building.

In case that heat gain exceeds the thermal capacity of the whole building, the energy flows to external seasonal heat storage, where it will be reserved for later reheating.

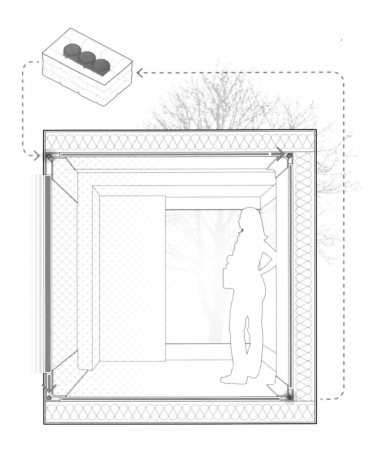

Heating cycle in winter

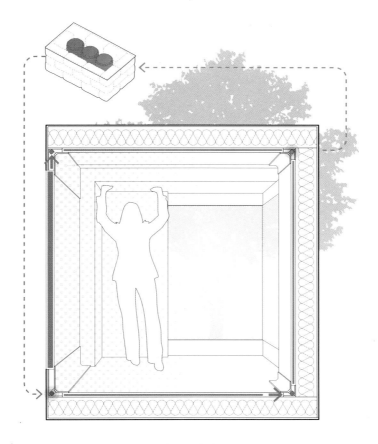

Cooling cycle (heat storage) in summer

Allwater Pavilion is a built experimental structure exploring potentials of trans-structure; however, it also takes the limitations of local climate and legislations into account. Heat absorption was limited to indoors due to necessary insulation at perimeter surface. Although the ideal solution would be to combine internal gains with the external surface and directly connect water with both sides, in this case the practical choice was to balance heat collection and heating energy demand by utilizing insulation on the perimeter surface due to consequent exterior energy loss. Allwater Pavilion in this sense combines embedded responsiveness of trans-structure with conventional building solution, proving that the concept can be effectively modified by local conditions as well for each project. This decision however should not be understood as a compromise but rather as an affordance of trans-structure concept.

IN ADDITION TO THE IMPORTANCE OF BEING A BUILT HYBRID TRANS-STRUCTURE AND WATER HOUSE, ALLWATER PAVILION VIVIDLY SHOWS THE EFFECT AND POTENTIAL OF TRANS-STRUCTURE. SEVERAL FUNDAMENTAL DESIGN CONSIDERATIONS OF A CONVENTIONAL BUILDING ARE REVERSED HERE.

The structure works as a heat collector and is exposed to heat gain as much as possible (which would be normally completely undesirable), since heat load here is not an encumbrance but an opportunity.

With effective distribution, fundamental aspects of sustainable design, like orientation, transparent surface proportion of facades, become less determining for energy consumption or thermal comfort.
Trans-structure in this respect provides more freedom in architectural design, since the perceived limitations to be avoided are converted into generative forces of embedded responsiveness in the building.

Such responsiveness is not merely an underlying hidden performance system but a perceivable evident flow. Transparency possesses a new dimension by presenting the contained space and the maintaining processes "physically" and "phenomenally" simultaneously. The water flow fuses these two aspects physically through transparent panel and phenomenally by creating different transparency modes based on microclimatic demands. This 'Performative Transparency' mutually affects and affected by spatial experience as much as by the behavior of the structure itself.

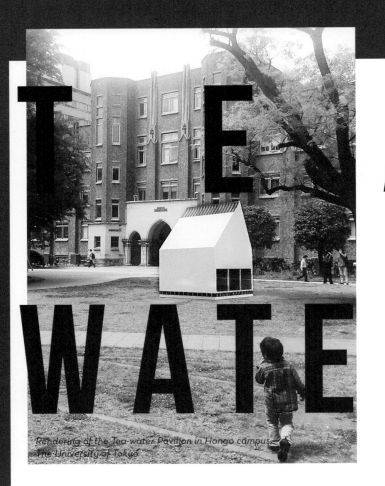

TEA WATER

PAVILION

Rendering of the Tea-water Pavilion in Hongo campus,
The University of Tokyo

TEA-WATER PAVILION
WHEN BRICKS ARE DROPS

Brick is the first building material created by men: the walls
in cities of Tell Aswad and Diyarbakir are more than 9500
years old. These ancient settlements (together with Jericho,
Catal Hüyük and Chogha Zanbil) are among earliest traces of
human civilization as well. Brick is as old as architecture.
Brick is symbol and source of power and authority. Leaders,
kings and builders marked their accomplishments perpetual
through them. For a long time, bricks defined architecture and
building, not only construction, but also planning and design.
When Kanto earthquake hit modern Japan in 1923, most of
the buildings including the new brick structures in Tokyo
area were destroyed. Imperial Hotel designed by Frank Lloyd
Wright survived, and the age of reinforced concrete building
started in Japan. The common faith of strength against
the forces of nature ruled modern architecture in Japan
for almost a century. Tohoku earthquake and the waves of
tsunami in 2011 washed away this belief and made Japanese
architects to reconsider their relationship with nature.
The age of brick and strength in architecture was at the verge
of inherent change.

TEA-WATER PAVILION IS AN ATTEMPT TO FIND NEW STRENGTH IN RESPONSIVENESS INSTEAD OF PASSIVE FORCE. BASED ON THIS NEW PROPERTY, THE BUILDING ALSO REDEFINES HUMAN-NATURE RELATIONSHIP BETWEEN BUILDING AND ENVIRONMENT.

The pavilion is a joint research project between private companies (Mitsubishi Plastics and Asahi Glass) and laboratories in the University of Tokyo. This micro pavilion is 4.5 tatami mat size space (about 7.3 m^2 or 70 sq. foot) for tea ceremonies. Designed with simple shape of a house, the aluminum skin has openings only in the top and on the east-west sides, where the entrances will be located. Following Japanese tradition, the height of the entrance is only about 90 cm (nijiriguchi), which served in history as a symbol of social equality, due to its modest proportions.

The building envelope is made to serve the water house energy model and to enclose a space with a unique atmosphere. The pitched roof is determined by the angle of insolation to maximize the heat absorption of aluminum-water panels. The openings at top and bottom are defined to keep close relation to surrounding nature, while lights and shadows characterize the space inside. Gravel floor is selected to maintain effective thermal comfort with water layer beneath, and local stones from riverbed are selected to invite Nature inside the building.

With a thin perimeter skin, Tea-Water Pavilion defines a space with intensive connection to Nature, surrounded by water in visible-hidden and enclosed-open states.

*Rendering of the Tea-water Pavilion in Hongo campus
The University of Tokyo*

The building will be exhibited in Hongo campus of the University of Tokyo after completion. Later the pavilion will be transported and rebuilt in Fukushima area and offered as gift for refugees who are still unable to return to their habitat. The multigenerational families, who used to live mostly in the same villages or households, were forced to move into temporary housings provided for single occupants, which could hardly accommodate their lifestyle. Young members left for larger cities while elderly stayed in the housings prepared by the government.

Tea-Water Pavilion is therefore more than a gift for the refugees: it provides them a new type of space to empower their community and help them to reconnect with their family members by providing a space for a meaningful ceremony in Japanese culture and tradition.

CLIMATE CONDITIONS ARE ESSENTIAL FOR ARCHITECTURE AND THERMAL COMFORT, WHERE THE UTILIZED ENERGY MODELS ARE UNIVERSAL. IN CASE OF TRANS-STRUCTURE, HOWEVER THE ENERGY MODEL VARIES FOR EACH LOCATION WHILE THE STRUCTURE ITSELF IS IN CONSTANT TRANSITION FROM ONE STATE TO THE OTHER.

The energy model applied for Japan is very different from the one developed for Allwater pavilion (in continental climate, in the previous chapter) not only because of climate, but also because of legislative limitations.

In case of continental climate, insulation has to be used for perimeter structure and the pavilion therefore collects heat surplus indoors. Winter solar insolation is also not sufficient to maintain thermal comfort thus solar storage is necessary to reserve the summer gain for the winter. In case of Japan however, there is no such limitation, especially because solar gain is relatively high for the whole year, while temperatures are also milder compared to Middle-Europe.

These conditions give the opportunity to set an even more ambitious goal than for the Allwater pavilion in Hungary by building a new sustainable and energy-efficient building without any insulation. This solution takes one step closer to the ideal trans-structure: energy absorption instead of thermal resistance, reaction instead of passive isolation. The comparison of a wall in a low energy house (about 50 cm) with the one of Tea-water pavilion (5 cm) vividly shows that trans-structures are not simply more efficient systems or upgrades of existing solutions, but rather an unprecedented building system which redefines the role of the building envelope and the interior-exterior spatial relationship.

Tea-Water Pavilion is built of prefabricated panels, which contain the water itself. The fluid volumes are connected through special joint units to unite the whole perimeter skin in one large water volume. Diagram shows the section of the pavilion during cooling and heating periods: solar heat gain is directly absorbed in the building skin; the aluminum surface conducts the solar gain directly to the water inside.

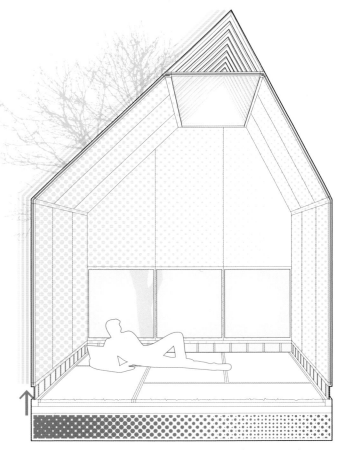

*Tea-water Pavilion energy diagram,
Heating cycle*

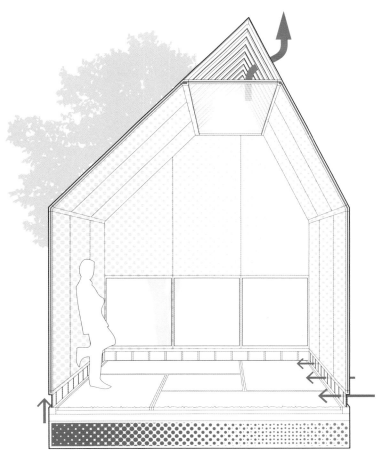

*Tea-water Pavilion energy diagram,
Cooling (heat storage) cycle*

The stored heat flows into a large water tank below the building, which also serves as foundation as well. The tank stores enough energy to heat the building for one week, which is the longest anticipated period without sufficient solar recharge in winter. The water storage supplies energy in the heating periods. The energy flow is led by thermal conduction and convection: the heat surplus moves to colder areas and maintain perfect balance and ideal temperature for both indoor air and surfaces. The installed pump and monitoring system is therefore only necessary in case of peak loads.

Tea-Water Pavilion project was led by Kengo Kuma Laboratory at the University of Tokyo. Three other laboratories joined the research project in the university: Prof. Tomonari Yashiro with Asst. Prof. Yu Morishita and Prof. Bumpei Magori of engineering and Asst. Prof. Jun Sato of structure, were key contributors in the design process. Mitsubishi Plastics (supplier of aluminum panel Alpolic) and Asahi Glass (supplier of glass materials) supported the project and the research. The panels were tested in the structure laboratory of Prof. Sato in University of Tokyo: shear tests conducted on both glass-steel and aluminum-steel panels determined the combined structural strength and behavior of the hybrid system.

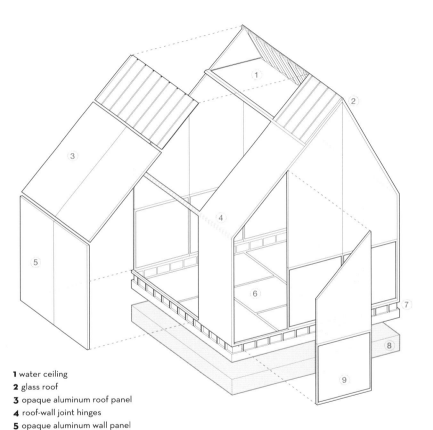

1 water ceiling
2 glass roof
3 opaque aluminum roof panel
4 roof-wall joint hinges
5 opaque aluminum wall panel
6 local stone gravel floor in tatami frames
7 bottom hinges
8 water foundation and heat storage
9 glass panel with water layer (bottom),
opaque panel (top)

Tea-water Pavilion isometric

The pavilion system consists of opaque and transparent panels (roof, wall and floor). The layout of each panel is very similar, regardless of its position. The building is isolated from the foundation and heat storage, but the fluid volume is interconnected with valves and joint elements. The panels are designed with structural frame and hinges in order to connect them directly to each other. The hinges also provide void between, which is necessary to join the water volumes of each panel. The hinges bring another important advantage as well: by elevating the building from the ground, light enters the space from the lowest point, where wall meets the floor. In addition to the low light, a glass ceiling is the other source of illumination, with a water surface, where condensation takes place to cool the space.

The drops falling on the thin water layer remind us on the passage of time and elements of nature to enhance the tea ceremony experience. 'Performative Transparency' delivers Lightness that is demarcated regarding to both heaviness and darkness. The spatial quality is defined by transitional stability of the structure as well as the balancing processes flowing on the building envelope.

———————————————————

ENDNOTES

Sustainability changed architecture and design in many ways in the past and its inherent challenges can still instigate a new paradigm in design thinking today. Regardless of social, cultural or structural point of view, buildings arguably aspired to be statement of stability as an end product.

Trans-structures in this respect seek new ways of stability as process resulting in qualities like 'Performative Transparency' and Stability of constant transition.
The projects presented here are novel attempts toward resilience-based design thinking, which utilizes embedded responsiveness of materials and structure. Trans-structure in this sense does not merely overwrite the existing or the past: it rather aims to enrich architecture with a new design strategy in which new material combinations and structural properties take shape in an innovative and sustainable design method for our time and the future to come.

ACKNOWLEDGEMENTS

Water House and Trans-structure research was conducted at
The University of Tokyo, initially at the Laboratory of Prof. Kazuhiko
Namba as a PhD research, and later as a Postdoc research at the
Prof. Kengo Kuma Lab. I am truly grateful and honoured by their
support. I would like to thank three partner laboratories: Asst. Prof.
Jun Sato of structure, Prof. Tomonari Yashiro, Prof. Bumpei Magori
and Asst. Prof. Yu Morishita of engineering in Tea-water Pavilion
project respectfully. Additionally, I am thankful for the help of
Prof. Jeno Kontra and Prof. Janos Varfalvi at Budapest University
of Technology and Economics Department of Building Energetics
for the tests on Allwater Panel prototypes. I am truly in debt of
Japanese Society for the Promotion of Science for their financial
support on this project and for the support of Quatro Sport Ltd and
EU Research Grant for Allwater Pavilion project. I am truly thankful
for Mitsubishi Plastics and Asahi Glass Corporation for their support
on Tea-water Pavilion project.

Finally, this book itself is not an achievement of one author, but of a
group of talented friends. I feel deeply in debt to Liliana Rodrigues
(graphic design), Aris Kafantaris (illustrations) and Zoheir Mottaki
(academic editing) as core team members of this book. Additionally
I would like to thank Jenny Kan and Jagoda Krawczyk (Pattern
Panel), Ana Ilic (interview editing), Rafael Balboa and Ilze Paklone
(editing guidance) for their integral contributions and remarkable
dedicated assistance. I was honoured to have them all on my
journey for trans-structure.